PRAYING IN THE PRESENCE OF

# OUR LORD

## WITH THE
## SAINTS

# PRAYING IN THE PRESENCE OF
# OUR LORD

## WITH THE SAINTS

FR. BENEDICT J. GROESCHEL, C.F.R.
AND JAMES MONTI

Our Sunday Visitor Publishing Division
Our Sunday Visitor, Inc.
Huntington, Indiana 46750

*Nihil Obstat*: Francis J. McAree, S.T.D.
Censor Librorum
*Imprimatur*: ✠ Robert A. Brucato, D.D.
Vicar General, Archdiocese of New York
December 19, 2000

Most of the Scripture verses cited in this work are taken from the *Revised Standard Version, Catholic Edition*, copyright © 1965 and 1966 by the Division of Christian Education of the National Council of the Churches of Christ in the U.S.A. and are used by permission of the copyright owner. The authors and publisher are grateful to those publishers and others whose materials, whether in the public domain or protected by copyright laws and cited throughout, have been included in this work. Every reasonable effort has been made to determine copyright holders. If any copyrighted materials have been inadvertently used without proper credit being given in one manner or another, please notify Our Sunday Visitor in writing so that future editions may be corrected accordingly.

Our Sunday Visitor Publishing Division
Our Sunday Visitor, Inc.
200 Noll Plaza
Huntington, IN 46750

ISBN: 0-87973-948-7
LCCCN: 00-111639

Cover design by Tyler Ottinger
Interior design by Sherri L. Hoffman

PRINTED IN THE UNITED STATES OF AMERICA

✠

To Our Lady of the Blessed Sacrament,
Queen of All Saints.

# *Acknowledgments*

✠

We wish to express our gratitude to the staffs of the Corrigan Memorial Library of Saint Joseph's Seminary, Yonkers, New York, and Marymount Library of Tarrytown, New York, for making available to us their collections of books and periodicals. We also wish to thank Sister Maria McCall, S.B.S., of the Archives of the Blessed Sacrament Sisters, Bensalem, Pennsylvania, for providing us with texts of the prayers of St. Katharine Drexel.

All prayers and meditations not cited in the "Sources for Texts" have been provided by the editorial staff of Our Sunday Visitor.

# Table of Contents

✠

# Introduction I

*Spending an Hour with Our Lord:*
*What to Do After You Kneel Down*

✠

---

## By Father Benedict J. Groeschel, C.F.R.

$\mathcal{A}$s devotion to Christ present in the Holy Eucharist has spread throughout the Church, and literally hundreds of thousands are trying to spend an hour with Him at prayer, the question arises, "What do I do with this hour?" Our book *Praying in the Presence of Our Lord: Prayers for Eucharistic Adoration* (Our Sunday Visitor, 1999) was very well received and has given rise to the request for more. In the present volume, James Monti has researched a fascinating collection of prayers and meditations of saints, blesseds, those declared Venerable, and Servants of God who left us their own written Eucharistic devotions. Although not all are specifically for the quiet contemplative exercise of a Holy Hour, all can be helpful for that precious time when we go apart with Christ for a while.

Because we are concerned to be a practical help with this book, I decided to spend a few pages indicating a simple and effective way of praying in silent adoration and contemplation — a way that does not presume either great experience or depth of knowledge about prayer. Actually, I discussed this method more extensively in my little book *Listening at Prayer* (Paulist Press, 1984). The following are a series of simple steps based on a method of St. Teresa of Avila, who said that she was afraid to go into prayer without a book in her hands. If St. Teresa used a book, we can hardly do better than to follow her lead.

**Step I:** Collect your thoughts in an act of remembrance and adoration of the One you are about to speak to. We need to break the rapidly flowing stream of consciousness that has accompanied us through the day and brought us to the threshold of the chapel where Christ awaits us in His mysterious sacramental presence. Simply put, you have to stop and remind yourself that you are going to pray — you are going to speak with Jesus Christ, your Lord and Redeemer, present in His Body and Blood, Soul and Divinity, as He was at Bethlehem, Nazareth, Jerusalem, and as He now is in eternal life and glory. The first step of real devotion is to be deeply aware that Christ is present to you, that He knows you and cares about you.

To stop the flow of everyday thoughts, it is helpful to kneel in adoration, and to take some deep breaths that help to calm us down and to repeat inwardly, "I am here with my Savior and my God," or some similar expression of the awe we ought to experience in His presence. After all, we are talking to God. One should spend as much time as one needs to do this. To be effective, it really takes several minutes. Frankly, I think that those who minimize the importance of kneeling simply lack the experience of awe.

At the end of this step, taking a couple of minutes of complete silence is helpful, but this should be discontinued if the mind begins to wander and be filled with distracting thoughts. The end of the period of silence should be a fervent appeal to the Holy Spirit to give us the grace to pray well and in union with Christ.

**Step II:** Now find a prayer or meditation or two in this book or some other book of devotion. This might best be accompanied by one of the citations from the Scriptures given in Appendix 2. Or better, keep your Bible with you if it is marked with quotations that you like.

Take time to find the quotation that fits your need at the moment. This should be a matter of what catches your attention and is based on your need in the situation that you have been in during this day.

Read the quotation a few times, savor it, and let its meaning fill your mind. Compare the truth or sentiment of the quotation with your present mood or need or state of mind. For example, if you are anxious about some specific thing in your life, many quotations from the psalms will be helpful to you. For instance, Psalm 107, from verse 4 to verse 9, gives us an image of God feeding the troubled soul and satisfying the soul's hunger and thirst. This obviously can be related easily to the experience of receiving Holy Communion.

**Step III:** Allow the meaning of the quotation or prayer to sink into your mind and heart. This may not feel very elevating, and it may be very silent. Let the quotation sink in quietly. Don't be afraid to take some time just allowing the words to enter into your mind and heart.

**Step IV:** Then, in your own words and thoughts, speak to Our Lord, recalling His presence with such sentiments as awe, joy, gratitude, sorrow for sin, trust. Don't be afraid to express fear, disappointment, frustration, and confusion. This is part of the purification we must sometimes enter into in the presence of the Savior of the World. Sentiments can be best expressed in very simple individual phrases like the following:

> Jesus, I adore You, Son of God.
> Jesus, I am so grateful to You.
> Jesus, I am filled with joy that You are with me.
> Jesus, I hurt very badly.
> Jesus, what went wrong?
> Jesus, why did I fall and fail?
> Jesus, I am hurt and angry.
> Jesus, I don't understand.
> Jesus, increase my faith.
> Jesus, be with me in my troubles.
> Jesus, keep me with Your cross.
> Jesus, don't leave me.
> Jesus, be with those I love and care about.

These are just a few of the sentiments we might express. Obviously, there are hundreds of different ones. Remember that you can say anything to Jesus Christ in such an intimate moment.

As you come to an end of such expressions, see if you can put all your feelings and experiences into a simple prayer, even a prayer without words.

Then, if there is time left, begin Step II again. This time, perhaps you should seek another Scripture quotation, perhaps a psalm of praise like 149 or 150; or if it is a difficult time, perhaps a psalm of repentance like Psalm 51. You can also seek for another prayer in this manual or some similar devotional book.

**Step V — Ending a Holy Hour:** As loyal disciples of Christ, we always ought to end our prayer with some resolution of charity, some decision to let Christ operate in our lives, so that each day it may be more and more true that "it is no longer I who live, but Christ who lives in me" (Gal 2:20).

We should think of some realistic action that we should take to show our love for Jesus by serving His brothers and sisters for whom He died. What we do to others we do to Him.

To act in a way that is realistically united with His life of grace, we must proceed from a Christian motive and do things in a way that reflects His Gospel example and teaching. We never do this perfectly, but we can pray and struggle to do it better.

I came long ago to suspect any Christian prayer or experience that does not lead to Christlike action. "If you love me, keep my commandments. . . . As you did it to one of the least of these my brethren, you did it to me. . . . I was hungry and you gave me food" (Jn 14:15; Mt 25:40; Mt 25:35). The honesty of prayer can be judged by the actions and struggles of grace as we surrender to the call of the Holy Spirit sent into our souls by our Blessed Master to teach us all that we need to know.

I always spend the last few moments of this time with Christ, asking the help and protection of His Mother and our Mother. I also address a few saintly friends already in the Kingdom of God and ask them to pray for me. And, finally, I greet my guardian angel, that mysterious celestial citizen whom God gave me when I started out on this brief human experience. I almost always leave the presence of Our Lord refreshed or at least better prepared for whatever the day may bring.

✝ ✝ ✝

*I bring to Mass today:*
— *my hopes and my needs, my trials, and my fears;*
— *my gratitude for all that I have received from my Father's hand up to the present moment;*
— *my desire to remain close to my Father and come even closer to him during this day.*
*I come to the altar today:*
— *to give thanks for the daily mystery of my redemption and salvation;*
— *to seek the strength and perseverance that I find so lacking in myself;*
— *to seal again the covenant with God, my Father, in and through Christ Jesus my Lord.*

— THE SERVANT OF GOD
TERENCE CARDINAL COOKE (1921–1983)[1]

# Introduction II

*The Holy Eucharist: The Inestimable Gift of Christ*

## By James Monti

*T*he early twentieth-century Italian mystic St. Gemma Galgani once described the Mass as the "Academy of Paradise" where we "learn to love"; indeed, it is from the Eucharist that every saint down through the centuries has learned the love of God and neighbor. From the recorded prayers and reflections of the saints and from the accounts of their lives, we in turn are able to learn what they learned from the Blessed Sacrament. The present work attempts to bring together the collected Eucharistic wisdom of the innumerable men and women who have responded to God's love with all their love. Of the utmost importance in this collection are the prayers the saints addressed to Our Lord in the Blessed Sacrament — these texts afford us the opportunity to make their words a part of our own conversation with Christ in the Eucharist.

The gift of the Eucharist is given to us in three ways — as the re-presentation of the Sacrifice of Calvary in the Mass, as our spiritual nourishment in the reception of Holy Communion, and as the abiding presence of our Savior in the reserved Sacrament. Parallel to these three dimensions of the Blessed Sacrament are our responses to this gift — preparation, thanksgiving, and adoration. Hence, the present work is divided into three corresponding sections, offering the prayers, thoughts, and actions of the saints in preparing for Mass and Holy Communion, in thanksgiving for Holy Communion, and in the prolonged dialogue with God that characterizes Eucharistic adoration outside of Mass. From these three dimensions of Eucharistic worship we learn how the saints became saints. The secret to sanctity can be found in the twenty or thirty minutes it takes to attend daily Mass and receive Holy Communion and, at the end of the day, in stepping out of the world into the silent presence of our Savior in the tabernacle for whatever length of time we are able to offer Him, even if it be no more than a minute or two.

In addition to many texts from the writings and lives of the canonized saints, as well as those whom the Church has pronounced Blessed or who have been declared Venerable by her, there is at the conclusion of each section of the present work a closing reflection drawn from various sources — from anonymous early and medieval texts, as well as from the writings of prominent Catholics including Servants of God whose causes have been introduced but who as of this time have not been declared Venerable. Additional materials of this nature are provided in Appendix 1, to serve as supplemental sources of reflection upon the Blessed Sacrament.

In view of the desire of Pope John Paul II for the rapid advancement of many candidates to beatification and canonization, we have deemed it appropriate to include those who have been declared Venerable as well as a few Servants of God in this work. Nonetheless, in loving obedience and fidelity to the decrees of Pope Urban VIII and other popes in regard to sainthood, the authors fully acknowledge and declare that the final judgment of the sanctity of those who have not yet been canonized rests with the Church alone.

Each section is divided into "Prayers" and "Meditations," within which the texts are given in chronological order according to the date of birth of the saint or blessed or candidate declared Venerable. All individuals are introduced with a title indicating their state of life as well as the country or countries where they lived at least a part of their lives. Please note that in addition to prayers addressed explicitly to Our Lord in the Blessed Sacrament, some prayers have been included that are addressed to Christ without a specific Eucharistic context — as the primary purpose of this book is devotional, such prayers have been utilized because they are certainly appropriate to Eucharistic worship regardless of their original context.

It is the hope and prayer of both Father Benedict and I that the present work may serve as a further instrument in the renewal of Eucharistic devotion with which God has blessed the Church in our time.

＋ ＋ ＋

*Hail Lord Jesus Christ, Word of the Father, Son of the Virgin, Lamb of God, Salvation of the world, Sacred Host, Word made Flesh, Fount of goodness.*

*Hail Lord Jesus Christ, Praise of angels, Glory of saints, Vision of peace, whole Godhead, true Man, Blossom and Fruit of the Virgin Mother.*

*Hail Lord Jesus Christ, Splendor of the Father, Prince of Peace, Gate of Heaven, Glory of the Kingdom, Living Bread, Born of the Virgin, Vessel of Divinity.*

*Hail Lord Jesus Christ, Light of Heaven, Foundation of the World, our Joy, Bread of Angels, Joy of the Heart, King and Spouse of Virginity.*

*Hail Lord Jesus Christ, sweet Way, pure Truth, supreme Love, our Reward, Fount of love, Peace of goodness, true Rest, everlasting Life, where after the present misery you may deign to refresh us with your face, who art God of gods, King of kings, and Lord of rulers, forever and ever. Amen.*

— FROM A FOURTEENTH-CENTURY
MANUSCRIPT OF ASSISI[2]

# I.

*Prayers and Meditations
Before Mass and
Holy Communion*

# Prayers

✠

## St. John Chrysostom

*Archbishop of Constantinople, Father of the Church*
*(Turkey, Armenia, Cappadocia: c. 347-407)*

O Christ,
Great and holiest Passover!
O Wisdom, Word, and Power of God!
Grant that we may receive you more perfectly
   in the day of your eternal kingdom.
May our lips be filled with your praise,
O Lord,
so that we may sing your glory;
for you have been pleased
to make us sharers in your holy, divine,
   immortal, and life-giving Mysteries.
Keep us in your holiness
so that all day long
we may learn your goodness.
We thank you, Lord, Lover of mankind,
   Benefactor of our souls,
because you have been pleased today
to make us sharers in your heavenly
and immortal Mysteries.
Make straight our paths.
Strengthen us in awesome reverence for you.

Guard our life,
Guide our steps,
    through the prayers and intercession
    of the glorious Mother of God,
    the ever-virgin Mary,
    and of all your saints.
Amen.

☩

## St. Bernard of Clairvaux

*Cistercian Monk, called "Last of the Fathers,"*
*titled "Doctor Mellifluous" (France: 1090-1153)*

Oh, how good and pleasant a thing it is
to dwell in the Heart of Jesus!
Who is there that does not love
a heart so wounded?
Who can refuse a return of love
to a heart so loving!
Amen.

☩

## St. Clare of Assisi

*Virgin, Co-foundress of the Franciscan Order*
*(Italy: 1194-1253)*

Praise and glory be to you, O loving Jesus Christ,
for the most sacred wound in your side . . .

and for your infinite mercy
which you made known to us in the opening
of your breast to the soldier Longinus,
and so to us all.

I pray you, O most gentle Jesus,
having redeemed me by baptism
    from original sin,
so now, by your Precious Blood,
    which is offered and received
    throughout the world,
deliver me from all evils,
past, present and to come.

And, by your most bitter death,
give me a lively faith,
    a firm hope, and
    a perfect charity,
so that I may love you
    with all my heart
    and all my soul,
    and all my strength;
make me firm and steadfast
    in good works
and grant me perseverance
    in your service
so that I may be able to please you always.
Amen.

✠

## St. Thomas Aquinas
*Priest, Dominican Scholar, Doctor of the Church,*
*Patron of Catholic Universities (Italy: 1225-1274)*

Almighty and ever-living God, I approach the sacrament of your only-begotten Son, our Lord Jesus Christ.

I come sick to the doctor of life, unclean to the fountain of mercy, blind to the radiance of eternal light, and poor and needy to the Lord of heaven and earth.

Lord, in your great generosity, heal my sickness, wash away my defilement, enlighten my blindness, enrich my poverty, and clothe my nakedness.

May I receive the Bread of angels, the King of kings and Lord of lords, with humble reverence, with the purity and faith, the repentance and love, and the determined purpose that will help to bring me to salvation.

May I receive the sacrament of the Lord's body and blood, and its reality and power.

Kind God, may I receive the body of your only-begotten Son, our Lord Jesus Christ, born from the womb of the Virgin Mary, and so be received into his mystical body and be numbered among his members.

Loving Father, as on my earthly pilgrimage I now receive your beloved Son under the veil of a sacrament, may I one day see him face to face in glory, who lives and reigns with you for ever and ever.

Amen.

*Also by St. Thomas:*

> O Sacred Banquet,
> in which Christ is received,
> the memory of his passion is renewed,
> the soul is filled with grace,
> and a pledge of future glory is given to us.

✠

## Bl. Margaret Ebner
*Virgin, Dominican Mystic (Germany: 1291-1351)*

Give us, my Lord, a sweet inner desire from a pure heart for the living food of your Holy Body and a loving thirst to receive you in accord with your innermost mercy; and undertake in us with sweetness a merciful work with full grace, so that we will perceive truly in ourselves the hidden power of your holy sacraments, ever acquiring virtues, ever increasing in grace.

And I ask you, my Lord, to feed us this day in union with the most worthy priest, who receives you today on earth. . . . By the grace of your presence may we feel no lack of you because of the sad state of

Christianity, and on that account may we never harm by evil the pure Truth, which is you yourself, O God, in whom all truth is seen. And may we appear before your divine face innocent of this sin and of all sins and well adorned with the fullness of all grace. May we be strengthened by your living food so that we increase in fiery love, be surrounded by your boundless mercy against all evil, and be embraced by your pure truth. . . .

My Lord, may your glorified, grace-filled humanity, Jesus Christ, be my innermost strength, a purification of my whole life, and an enlightening of all my senses to recognize the real and only truth. My surest way to you, my Lord, on the way of real truth must be for us the true light of your pure life of thirty-three years on earth, your humble deeds, your gentle course of life, your powerful suffering, your love-filled death, your true words.[3]

✠

## Bl. Peter Favre
*Jesuit Priest, Theologian (France, Italy: 1506-1546)*

O my Lord, I beg you to take from me whatever divides, separates, and distances me from you and you from me. . . . Take from me all that makes me unworthy of your visitation. . . .

Have mercy on me, O Lord, have mercy on me always; drive far from me all the evil in me which hinders me from beholding you; from hearing you

and delighting in you; from perceiving your fragrance
. . . from loving and possessing you; from abiding in
your presence and beginning to find delight in you.[4]

☦

---

## St. Louis Marie de Montfort
*Priest, Religious, Founder of Two Orders,*
*Apostle of Marian Devotion (France: 1673-1716)*

My Jesus, I long ardently
For you to come to me this day;
Without you life is misery.
Come to me soon, I pray.

Without the fervor that you bring,
O Love, I languish night and day;
And do you not desire my love?
Inflame my heart, I pray.

Good Shepherd, bear your lost sheep home
Within your arms, when e'er I stray;
From ravening wolves that round me roam
O keep me safe, I pray.

O Bread of Life, for you I sigh,
Give me yourself without delay;
For otherwise my soul must die.
Give me to eat, I pray.

O fount of living waters clear,
How long and weary is the way;

Refresh my soul which thirsts for you.
Give me to drink, I pray.

O loving Lord, my soul is chilled
By icy winds that round me play;
O fire of love, let me be filled
With warmth from you, I pray.

Like the blind man who cried to you:
Have mercy on me, Lord, I say,
O Mary's son, that I may see;
Increase my faith, I pray.

Lord, I am sick beyond all cure,
But with a word you can display
Your power; without you death is sure.
O heal me, Lord, I pray.

My Lord, I knock upon your door;
Your favors I can ne'er repay,
Yet in my want I beg for more.
Fulfill my needs, I pray.

I am not worthy, Lord, that you
Should come into my house today
As heavenly food; say but the word
And heal my soul, I pray.

Lord, you alone are my true friend,
My treasure which can ne'er decay;
All earthly joys do you transcend.
Do visit me this day.[5]

## St. Benedict Joseph Labre
*Layman, Pilgrim (France, Italy: 1748-1783)*

*Aspirations for receiving Holy Communion:*

My Good . . . my Good . . . my All . . . sole Object of my love. . . .O come . . . I desire you . . . I sigh after you . . . I wait for you . . . every little delay seems a thousand years. . . .Come, Lord Jesus, and delay not.[6]

✠

## St. Vincent Pallotti
*Priest, Religious, Founder of the Society of the Catholic Apostolate (Italy: 1798-1850)*

My God, my mercy, although I have deserved . . . to remain deprived of the Most Holy Eucharist on the most holy altars, still I trust that You, my Jesus and infinite God, will always allow me to stay near You, that You will allow me to take communion every day until the end of my life, that You will inspire in me the keenest presence of mind before the Most Holy Eucharist — as though it were in my breast as it is in the holy pyxes, and within me as food for my soul, so that its merciful effects might be measured infinitely — that You will give me the grace to increase the number of those who adore and participate in the Most Holy Eucharist, and that You will make mine a life of perpetual preparation, participation, and thanksgiving in the infinite fruits of the Most Holy Eucharist.[7]

## Ven. John Henry Cardinal Newman
*Convert from Anglicanism, Priest, Writer, and Apologist*
*(England: 1801-1890)*

Thou knowest, O my God, who madest us, that nothing can satisfy us but Thyself, and therefore Thou hast caused Thy own self to be meat and drink to us. O most adorable mystery! O most stupendous of mercies! Thou most Glorious, and Beautiful, and Strong, and Sweet, Thou didst know well that nothing else would support our immortal natures, our frail hearts, but Thyself; and so Thou didst take a human flesh and blood, that they, as being the flesh and blood of God, might be our life.

. . . How can I raise myself to such an act as to feed upon God? O my God, I am in a strait — shall I go forward, or shall I go back? I will go forward: I will go to meet Thee. I will open my mouth, and receive Thy gift. I do so with great awe and fear, but what else can I do? to whom should I go but to Thee? Who can save me but Thou? Who can cleanse me but Thou? Who can make me overcome myself but Thou? Who can raise my body from the grave but Thou? Therefore I come to Thee in all these my necessities, in fear, but in faith.

My God, Thou art my life; if I leave Thee, I cannot but thirst. . . . I wish to be clad in that new nature, which so longs for Thee from loving Thee, as to overcome in me the fear of coming to Thee. I come to Thee, O Lord, not only because I am unhappy without Thee, not only because I feel I need Thee, but because Thy grace draws me on to seek Thee for Thy own sake, because Thou art so glorious and beautiful. I come in great fear, but in greater love.[8]

✠

---

### St. Pius X

*Pope, urged frequent reception of Holy Communion and lowering the age for First Holy Communion (Italy: 1835-1914)*

O most sweet Jesus, who came into this world to give all souls the life of your grace, and who, to preserve and increase it in them, willed to be the daily Remedy of their weakness and the Food for each day, we humbly beseech you, by your heart so burning with love for us, to pour your divine Spirit upon all souls in order that those who have the misfortune to be in the state of mortal sin may, returning to you, find the life of grace which they have lost.

Through this same Holy Spirit, may those who are already living by this divine life devoutly approach your divine Table every day when it is possible, so that, receiving each day in Holy Communion the antidote of their daily venial sins and each day sustaining in themselves the life of your grace and thus ever purifying themselves the more, they may finally come to a happy life with you. Amen.

# Meditations

✝

## Bl. Angela of Foligno
*Third Order Franciscan, Mystic (Italy: c. 1248-1309)*

One should really do some serious thinking before going to receive the great favors accorded in this most high mystery. One should keep in mind whom one is approaching, what state one is in, and how and why one approaches it.

For one is going to a good which is the All Good, the cause of every good, the giver, producer, and possessor of every good. . . . This good suffices, fills, and satisfies all the saints and the blessed spirits, all the just justified by grace, and the souls and bodies of all the blessed who reign in glory.

One is also going to receive the Good, God-made-man, the one who satisfies, abounds, overflows, and enjoys himself in all creatures, above all creatures, and beyond all creatures, without mode or measure. . . .

One goes to this Good, beyond and outside of which there is no other good. O neglected, unknown, unloved Good, discovered by those who totally desire you and yet cannot possess you totally. If one looks and ponders with utmost care the small piece of bread which the body eats, how much more should the soul not look and ponder before receiving this eternal and infinite Good, created and uncreated, this sacramental food which is the sustenance, treasure, and fountain for the life of both soul and body. This is truly the Good which in itself contains every good. One must, therefore, approach such a table, and such a great and wonderful Good with great respect, purity, fear, and love. The soul must approach it all cleansed and adorned, because it is going to that which, and the one who, is the Good of all glory. It is going to that which, and the one who, is perfect blessedness, eternal life, beauty, loftiness, sweetness, all love and the sweetness of love.

Why should one go to this mystery? I will tell you what I think. One should go to receive in order to be received, go pure in order to be purified, go alive in order to be enlivened, go as just in order to be justified, go united and conjoined to Christ in order to be incorporated through him, with him, and in him, God uncreated and God-made-man, who is given in this most holy and most high mystery through the hands of the priest.[9]

✠

---

## St. Francis de Sales
*Bishop, Doctor of the Church (France: 1567-1622)*

Your great intention in receiving Communion should be to advance, strengthen, and comfort yourself in the love of God. You must receive with love that which love alone has caused to be given to you. . . .

If worldly people ask you why you receive Communion so often, tell them that it is to learn to love God, be purified from your imperfections, delivered from misery, comforted in affliction, and supported in weakness. . . . Tell them that for your part you are imperfect, weak, and sick and need to communicate frequently with him who is your perfection, strength, and physician.[10]

+ + +

We must never think that by going to Communion for others, or by praying for them, we lose anything. We need not fear that by offering to God this Communion or prayer in satisfaction for the sins of others, we shall not make satisfaction for our own. The merit of the Communion and of the prayer will remain with us.[11]

+

---

### Bl. Marie of the Incarnation
*Widow, Ursuline Religious, Missionary to the Native Americans of Canada (France, Canada: 1599-1672)*

This divine Shepherd, wishing to communicate his very self while giving communion to the Apostles, is filled with zeal — an ardent and burning zeal. "I have," he said, "desired with desire to eat this Pasch with you." This has shown me the disposition with which I should receive him. . . .

It seemed to me that he has left himself in the Holy Eucharist so that we would have under the veil of the sacred species what the saints have in full view and uncovered in heaven; and that as in heaven he is the paradise of the blessed, thus on earth he is also a paradise — but a hidden one — for pure souls who love him in truth.[12]

✠

### St. Madeleine Sophie Barat
*Virgin, Religious, Foundress of the Society of the Sacred Heart (France: 1779-1865)*

Ah! If we had faith! If we were penetrated by the thought that at this moment Our Lord is on the altar! We would be motionless, we would forget that we have bodies. . . . We have so much to ask for the Church, for sinners, for the Society, for our families, for the children entrusted to us, for ourselves.[13]

✠

### Ven. Francis Libermann
*Convert from Judaism, Priest, Superior of the Holy Ghost Fathers and Brothers (France: 1802-1852)*

*From a letter of Father Libermann to his niece Marie:*

Regarding frequent communion, I not only approve your desire, but strongly urge you to follow it.

Approach the Holy Table frequently and take care to prepare well for it. Convince yourself that if you stay away from the Bread of Angels, your soul will become weak and your fervor will diminish. Don't be afraid to go to communion! Our most sweet Savior is hidden among us on earth for the sole purpose of filling us with Himself. The more confidently we approach Him, the more lovingly He will receive us. If you receive this divine Sacrament frequently, you may be sure that you will persevere in piety. Moreover, if you are faithful to divine grace and strive to acquire solid virtues, you may be confident that this Sacrament will help you greatly and will make you reach solid perfection in a short time.[14]

## Bl. Frederick Ozanam
*Layman, Founder of the Society of St. Vincent de Paul, Catholic Writer (Italy, France: 1813-1853)*

*From three letters of Frederick Ozanam:*

When I have not been able to be with you on the great feast-days, I have found you at the altar. I believe firmly that, when I am receiving, I am in close touch with my friends, all united to the same Saviour.[15]

My dear friend, the Holy Communion in Notre Dame this morning was magnificent. Nearly two thousand were present, praising and blessing God and joining in the holy mysteries. It is indeed the truth that the merits of that Sacrifice are never exhausted, and that the Saviour is present to the faithful in His Church today, as in the early days of Christianity. I did not forget you, my dear friend, at the altar, and I am sure that you did not forget me.[16]

+ + +

In the inexpressible sweetness of Holy Communion and in the transport which it causes, there is a power for conviction which would enable me to embrace the Cross and defy unbelief, should all the world have abjured Christ.[17]

✠

---

## St. Bernadette Soubirous
*Virgin, Visionary of the Apparitions of the Blessed Virgin Mary at Lourdes, Religious (France: 1844-1879)*

[Regarding Holy Communion:] You must give God a good reception. We have every interest in welcoming Him for then He has to pay us for His lodging.[18]

## Ven. Matt Talbot
*Layman, Construction Worker, Third Order
Franciscan (Ireland: 1856-1925)*

Jesus Christ is at once the beginning, the way, and the immortal end which we must strive to gain, but above all in Holy Communion He is the Life of our souls.[19]

## Closing Reflection

*Picture then the High Priest Christ leaving the sacristy of heaven for the altar of Calvary. He has already put on the vestment of our human nature, the maniple of our suffering, the stole of priesthood, the chasuble of the Cross. Calvary is His cathedral; the rock of Calvary is the altar stone; the sun turning to red is the sanctuary lamp; Mary and John are the living side altars; the host is His Body; the wine is His Blood. He is upright as Priest, yet He is prostrate as Victim. His Mass is about to begin.*

— Archbishop Fulton J. Sheen
Writer, Homilist (United States: 1895-1979)[20]

# II.

## Prayers and Meditations for Thanksgiving Following Holy Communion

# Prayers

✠

---

## St. John Gualbert
*Benedictine, Founder of Twelve Monasteries*
*(Italy: 999-1073)*

*Prayer after Holy Communion:*

To you, Lord, I give thanks and praises. Preserve in me, Lord, an undefiled faith. To you I bow my head. To you I genuflect. You my Lord, one with [the Father and the Holy Spirit] in the Holy Trinity, I confess. Deliver me from dangers. Uphold me in all my causes. Lift me up from falling, and those things which I am not able to fulfill, grant as if they were prayed for. Amen.[21]

✠

---

## St. Thomas Aquinas
*Priest, Dominican Scholar, Doctor of the Church,*
*Patron of Catholic Universities (Italy: 1225-1274)*

Lord,
Father all-powerful and ever-living God,
I thank you,
    for even though I am a sinner,
    your unprofitable servant,

not because of my worth
    but in the kindness of your mercy
you have fed me with the precious body and blood
    of your Son, our Lord Jesus Christ.
I pray that this Holy Communion
    may not bring me condemnation
    and punishment,
but forgiveness and salvation.
May it be a helmet of faith
and a shield of good will.
May it purify me from evil ways
and put an end to my evil passions.
May it bring me charity and patience,
    humility and obedience,
    and growth in the power to do good.
May it be my strong defense
against all my enemies, visible and invisible,
and the perfect calming
    of all my evil impulses,
    bodily and spiritual.
May it unite me more closely to you,
the one true God,
and lead me safely through death
to everlasting happiness with you.
And I pray that you will lead me, a sinner,
to the banquet
where you, with your Son and Holy Spirit,
are true and perfect light,
total fulfillment,
everlasting joy,
gladness without end,

and perfect happiness to your saints.
Grant this through Christ our Lord.
Amen.

## Bl. Margaret Ebner
*Virgin, Dominican Mystic (Germany: 1291-1351)*

Lord, I praise you, true God and true man, and ask you, my Lord Jesus Christ, to forgive us all our sins and to take from us all natural defects by your love and grant us yourself with the full grace by which you accomplish your eternal honor in us now and forever!

I greet you, Lord of the whole world, only Word of the Father in heaven, only true sacrifice and only living flesh and only totally divine and truly human one. Give us love for you, true hope and perfect love, and strong, firm Christian faith in this life and at the hour of death.

I thank you, Lord Christ, that you have changed bread and wine into your Holy Body and Blood, that you, Lord Jesus Christ, have deigned in your love, to be offered to your Father by the priest to your eternal honor, and to console, to help and to sanctify us and all Christians living and dead. Now offer yourself today, Lord, for all the evil that we have done against you and for all the good that we have failed to do. And give yourself to us as a sure help in life and in death, and as true power with which we will be able to withstand all human evil by increasing in your heartfelt love.[22]

✠

---

## St. Mary Magdalen de' Pazzi
*Virgin, Carmelite (Italy: 1566-1607)*

All graces are contained in you, O Jesus in the Eucharist, our celestial Food! What more can a soul wish when it has within itself the One who contains everything? If I wish for charity, then I have within me Him who is perfect charity, I possess the perfection of charity. The same is true of faith, hope, purity, patience, humility, and meekness, for you form all virtues in our soul, O Christ, when you give us the grace of this Food. What more can I want or desire, if all the virtues, graces, and gifts for which I long, are found in you, O Lord, who are as truly present under the sacramental species as you are in heaven, at the right hand of the Father? Because I have and possess this great wonder, I do not long for, want, or desire any other![23]

✠

---

## St. Margaret Mary Alacoque
*Virgin, Visitation Nun*
*(France: 1647-1690)*

Jesus Christ, my Lord and my God, whom I believe to be really present in the Blessed Sacrament of the Altar, receive this most profound act of adoration to supply for the desire I have to adore You unceasingly, and in thanksgiving for the sentiments of love which Your Sacred Heart has for me in this sacrament.

I cannot better acknowledge them than by offering You all the acts of adoration, resignation, patience, and love which this same Heart has made during its mortal life, and which it makes still and which it shall make eternally in heaven, in order that through it I may love You, praise You, and adore You worthily as much as it is possible for me.

I unite myself to this divine offering which You made to Your Father, and I consecrate to You my whole being, praying You to destroy in me all sin and not to permit that I should be separated from You eternally. Amen.

☩

## St. Leonard of Port Maurice

*Priest, Franciscan Preacher, Promoter of the Devotion of the Way of the Cross (Italy: 1676-1751)*

My Jesus, it is but justice and common gratitude that I should give myself entirely to you, after you have given yourself entirely to me . . . I ought henceforward to remain yours. May these eyes, renewed by you, remain yours; may these ears, sanctified by you, remain yours; this taste, sanctified by you, may it be yours. You have sanctified all my senses; may they be yours, and so may they never again take pleasure in opposition to your divine Law. You have sanctified my memory; may it continually remember you. You have sanctified my will; may it never turn to love anything in preference to you. Unto you, then, from the very depth of my heart, I offer, as a perpetual holocaust, my body and my soul, my senses and my faculties, all that I have and am, as fully as I can. Burn, O fire divine, burn and consume, O love omnipotent, all in me which is not yours! Amen.[24]

✠

## St. Benedict Joseph Labre
*Layman, Pilgrim (France, Italy: 1748-1783)*

O my Lord Jesus, grant that I may mortify myself, and live in you; that I may take from your hands whatever may happen, of prosperity or adversity; that I may fight against myself, and follow you constantly, that I may always more and more desire to follow you; that I may flee from myself, and take refuge in you; that I may be worthy to be protected by you; that I may fear you, who are all-powerful; that I may fear myself, who am inclined to evil; that I may be of the number of your elect; that I may distrust myself, and confide in you; that I may obey everyone for the love of you; that nothing earthly may move me, but raise me towards you. Cast on me a benign look, which may excite me to love you; call me to you, that I may see you in heaven, and enjoy you as my possession for eternity.[25]

✠

## Ven. John Henry Cardinal Newman
*Convert from Anglicanism, Priest, Writer, Apologist*
*(England: 1801-1890)*

Most sacred, most loving
Heart of Jesus,
You are concealed in the Holy Eucharist,
And you beat for us still.
Now, as then, you say:
 "With desire I have desired . . ."
I worship you with all my best love and awe,
With fervent affection,
With my most subdued, most resolved will.
For a while you take up your abode within me.
O make my heart beat with your Heart!
Purify it of all that is earthly,
All that is proud and sensual,
All that is hard and cruel,
Of all perversity,
Of all disorder.
So fill it with you,
That neither the events of the day,
Nor the circumstances of the time,
May have the power to ruffle it;
But that in your love and your fear,
It may have peace.
Amen.

# Meditations

✠

---

## St. Frances of Rome
*Wife and Mother, Widow, Religious, Foundress of the Congregation of Oblates (Italy: 1384-1440)*

*From an ecstasy of St. Frances following Holy Communion, July 22, 1431:*

I was led into a vast splendor and from it again into another of much greater brilliancy. There was an altar there of rare beauty. . . . Outstretched upon the tabernacle lay a Lamb of dazzling whiteness. . . .

Then I heard the Lamb saying in a voice of great sweetness: "I am Love Who first filleth the soul with the fragrance of the delicious fruits which grow in the homeland of heaven. After I have communicated to the soul the perfume of these delectable fruits, then do I give it appetite for them and the taste of their sweetness. . . .

"I am Love Who crieth with a loud voice: If anyone be athirst, let him come unto Me and drink! I will give their fill to all who come in answer to My invitation. Behold, it is for that I have torn open My Heart, that I may receive you therein as though it were an inn."[26]

✠

## St. Thomas More

*Layman, Lord Chancellor of England, Catholic Writer and Apologist, Martyr (England: 1478-1535)*

Now when we have received our Lord and have Him in our body, let us not then let Him alone, and get us forth about other things, and look no more unto Him . . . but let all our business be about Him. Let us by devout prayer talk to Him, by devout meditation talk with Him. Let us say with the prophet . . . *I will hear what our Lord will speak within me.*

For surely if we set aside all other things, and attend unto Him, He will not fail with good inspirations to speak such things to us within us as shall serve to the great spiritual comfort and profit of our soul. And therefore let us with Martha provide that all our outward business may be pertaining to Him, in making cheer to Him, and to His company for His sake: that is to wit, to poor folk, of which He taketh every one, not only for His disciple, but also as for Himself. . . . And let us with Mary also sit in devout meditation, and hearken well what our Savior, being now our guest, will inwardly say unto us. Now have we a special time of prayer, while He that hath made us, He that hath bought us, He whom we have offended, He that shall judge us . . . is of His great goodness become our guest, and is personally present within us. . . . Let us not lose this time therefore, suffer not this occasion to slip, which we can little tell whether ever we shall get it again or never. Let us endeavor ourselves to keep Him still, and let us say with His two disciples that were going to the castle of Emmaus: *Mane nobiscum Domine,* Tarry with us good Lord, and then shall we be sure that He will not go from us, but if we unkindly put Him from us.[27]

✠

## St. Teresa of Avila
*Virgin, Religious, Foundress of the Discalced Carmelite Order, Doctor of the Church (Spain: 1515-1582)*

Whenever you receive Holy Communion, beg some gift from God for the sake of His great mercy in visiting your poor soul.[28]

✠

## Ven. Anne de Xainctonge
*Virgin, Religious, Educator, Foundress of the Society of St. Ursula of the Blessed Virgin (France: 1567-1621)*

In giving Himself during the Mass to all who approach the Holy Table, Our Divine Lord teaches in what way one ought to respond to this gift. . . . There is never a fervent communion save when, in a perfect exchange, we give body for body, heart for heart, life for life, soul for soul. . . . This happy exchange shows itself in the diminution of our passions, the moderation of our desires, the control of our senses, the increase of our desire to see God, a practical esteem and love for virtue, peace of soul, contempt of the world, and a relishing of God. . . .

The most beautiful prayer of thanksgiving is the amendment of our life. Without this amendment, our gratitude lasts only a quarter hour. With it, on the contrary, our thanksgiving is solid and lasting.[29]

+ + +

O Jesus, give me today and all the days of my life the memory of Your Holy Passion. Make me share in Your wounds, Your thorns, Your Cross.[30]

✝

## St. Louise de Marillac
*Widow, Religious, Foundress of the Daughters of Charity of St. Vincent de Paul and the Ladies of Charity (France: 1591-1660)*

The Holy Communion of the Body of Jesus Christ causes us to enter into possession of the Communion of Saints and the joys of Paradise.[31]

✠

## St. Elizabeth Ann Seton
*Wife and Mother, Widow, Religious, Foundress of the Sisters of Charity (United States: 1774-1821)*

*Elizabeth Seton's account of her First Holy Communion, March 25, 1805:*

At last, God is mine and I am His! Now let all go its round. I have received Him! The awful impressions of the evening before, fears of not having done all to prepare, and yet even the transports of confidence and hope in His goodness. My God! to the last breath of life, will I not remember this night of watching for morning's dawn, the fearful beating heart so pressing to be gone, the long walk to town, but every step counted nearer that street, then nearer that Tabernacle, then nearer the moment He would enter the poor, poor little dwelling so all His own.

And when He did, the first thought I remember was: "Let God arise! Let His enemies be scattered!" For it seemed to me my King had come to take His throne, and instead of the humble, tender welcome I had expected to give Him, it was but a triumph of joy and gladness that the Deliverer was come, and my defense and shield, and strength and salvation made mine for this world and the next.

Now, then, all the transports of my heart found play . . . truly, I feel all the powers of my soul held fast by Him who came with so much majesty to take possession of His little poor kingdom.[32]

*From another of Mother Seton's writings:*

Oh, heavenly bliss! Delight past all expression! How consoling, how sweet, the presence of Jesus to the longing, harassed soul! It is instant peace and balm to every wound!

What would be my refuge? Jesus is everywhere. . . . Yes, everywhere! But in His Sacrament of the Altar, as actually present and real as my soul within my body. In His sacrifice, daily offered, as really as once offered on the cross. Merciful Savior! Can there be any comparison to this blessedness? Adored Lord, increase my faith, perfect it, crown it; Thine own, Thy choicest, dearest gift. Having drawn me from the pit, and drawn me to Thy fold, keep me in Thy sweet pastures and lead me to eternal life.

Jesus then is there. We can go, receive Him. He is our own. Were we to pause and think of this through eternity, yet we can only realize it by His conviction. Then He is there. Oh, heavenly theme! As entirely true as that bread naturally taken removes my hunger, so this Bread of Angels removes my pain, my cares; warms, cheers, soothes, contents, and renews my whole being.

Merciful God, and I do possess you! Kindest, tenderest, dearest friend! Every affliction of my nature absorbed in you still is active, nay, perfected in its operations through your refining love. Hush, my soul, we cannot speak it! Tongues of angels could not express our treasure of peace and contentment in Him.

O my soul, when our corrupted nature overpowers, when we are sick of ourselves, weakened on all sides, discouraged with repeated relapses, wearied with sin and sorrow, we gently, sweetly lay the whole account at His feet. Reconciled and encouraged by His appointed representative, yet trembling and conscious of our imperfect dispositions, we draw near the sacred fountain. Scarcely the expanded heart receives its longing desire, when wrapt in His love, covered with His righteousness, we are no longer the same. Adoration, thanksgiving, love, joy, peace, contentment! Let us always whisper His Name of love as an antidote to all the discord that surrounds us![33]

## St. Vincent Pallotti
*Priest, Religious, Founder of the Society of the Catholic Apostolate (Italy: 1798-1850)*

How did you prepare yourself for the most holy sacrament of the Eucharist? How did you make your thanksgiving? Did you receive the Eucharist as often as you could? And in the many times you received it, how well did you profit from it? When you received Jesus in the Blessed Sacrament, did you try to imitate Him in the virtues He practiced? How did you imitate Him in obedience . . . in charity towards all, modesty, humility, simplicity . . . whole-hearted work, prayer?[34]

✠

## Bl. Elizabeth of the Trinity
*Virgin, Carmelite Mystic (France: 1880-1906)*

*From a letter of Elizabeth to her mother:*

I am so glad that you are receiving Communion more often. It is there, my little Mama, that you will find strength. It is so good to think that after Communion we possess all of Heaven within our soul except the vision![35]

✠

## Bl. Pier-Giorgio Frassati
*Layman, University Student (Italy: 1901-1925)*

Jesus comes to visit me each morning in Holy Communion. I return His visit to Him in the poor.[36]

## Closing Reflection

*We give you thanks, O Christ, our God,*
*because you have deigned to share with us*
*your Body and your Blood, O Saviour;*
*you have drawn to yourself our hearts. . . .*

— FROM AN EARLY CHRISTIAN
EGYPTIAN OSTRACON INSCRIPTION[37]

# III.

## Prayers and Meditations for Visiting the Blessed Sacrament

# Prayers

✠

## St. Ignatius of Antioch
*Bishop of Antioch, Church Father (Syria: died c. 107)*

I am God's wheat; I am ground by the teeth of the wild beasts that I may end as the pure bread of Christ. . . .

I have no taste for the food that perishes, nor the pleasures of this life. I want the Bread of God, which is the Flesh of Christ, who was the seed of David; and for drink I desire His Blood which is love that cannot be destroyed.

✠

## St. Ephraem the Deacon
*Opposed the heresies of his time and was called the "Deacon of Edessa" (Syria: 306-373)*

God of God, true God of true God, we know that You are goodness itself. Assist us in Your benevolence. Protect us lest we some day share with Satan the pains of hell. Spread over us the wings of Your mercy.

We acknowledge You as the light; we are but servants in Your hands. Permit not that the evil one wrest us from You forever and that we rebel against Your sovereignty.

We know that You are just; be for us justice, O Lord. We know that You are our Savior; deliver and preserve us from evil. We proclaim Your holiness; sanctify us with Your Body and Blood. May the elect, who have eaten Your Flesh and drunk Your precious Blood, sing Your glory.

Grant us pardon, O God of goodness. You who are merciful to sinners. Amen.

✠

---

## St. Basil the Great
*Bishop of Caesarea, considered the
Father of Monasticism in the Eastern Churches
(Caesarea, Turkey: c. 329–379)*

We give You thanks, O Lord our God, for the Communion of Your holy, pure, and heavenly Mysteries, which You have given for the good, the hallowing and the healing of souls and bodies.

Do You, O Sovereign of the world, cause this Communion in the Holy Body and Blood of Your Christ to nourish in us unashamed faith, sincere charity, ripe wisdom, health of soul and body, separation from all ills, observance of Your Law and justification before His awful judgment seat.

O Christ our God, the mystery of Your Providence has been accomplished according to our ability. We have been reminded of Your death and we have seen a figure of Your Resurrection; we have been filled with Your infinite life and we have tasted Your inexhaustible joy; we pray You to make us worthy of these things in the life to come through the grace of Your eternal Father and of Your holy, good, and life-giving Spirit, now and forever, eternally. Amen.

⊹

---

## St. Columban
*Irish Monk, Scholar, founded monasteries in Western Europe (Ireland: 545-615)*

Merciful God, good Lord, I wish You would unite me to that fountain from which I might drink of the living spring of the water of life with those others who thirst after You. There in that heavenly region may I ever dwell, delighted with abundant goodness, and say, "How sweet is the fountain of living water which never falls, the water welling up into eternal life."

O God, You Yourself are that fountain, ever to be desired, ever to be consumed. Lord Christ, always give us this water to be for us the source of life. I ask You for Your great benefits.

You are our all: our life and our light, our food and our drink, our salvation and our God.

✠

## St. John Gualbert
*Benedictine, Founder of Twelve Monasteries*
*(Italy: 999-1073)*

*To the Son:* Have mercy, Lord, have mercy, O Christ, that you may teach me your holy will, that you may sustain me. You my Mercy, have mercy on me, that I may ably beseech you. Have mercy, Lord, have mercy, O Christ, that you may make me worthy to be heard favorably. Have mercy, Lord, have mercy, O Christ, that I may believe in you. Have mercy, Lord, have mercy, O Christ, that I may know you, that I may hope in you, and that I may love you, that my soul may live in you. Amen.[38]

✠

## St. Anselm of Canterbury
*Benedictine Abbot of the French Monastery of Bec,*
*Archbishop of Canterbury, Doctor of the Church*
*(Italy, France, England: 1033-1109)*

Lord, because you have made me, I owe you the whole of my love; because you have redeemed me, I owe you the whole of myself; because you have promised so much, I owe you all my being. . . . I pray you, Lord, make me taste by love what I taste by knowledge; let me know by love what I know by understanding. I owe you more than my whole self, but I have no more, and by myself I cannot render the whole of it to you. Draw me to you, Lord, in the fullness of love. I am wholly yours by creation; make me all yours, too, in love.

Lord, my heart is before you. I try, but by myself I can do nothing; do what I cannot. Admit me into the inner room of your love. I ask, I seek, I knock. You who made me seek, make me receive; you who gave the seeking, give the finding; you who taught the knocking, open to my knock. To whom will you give, if you refuse my petition? Who finds, if this seeking is in vain? To whom is it opened, if to this knocking it is closed? . . . Good Lord, do not reject me; I faint with hunger for your love; refresh me with it. Let me be filled with your love, rich in your affection, completely held in your care. Take me and possess me wholly, who with the Father and the Holy Spirit are alone blessed to ages of ages. Amen.[39]

✠

---

## St. Bernard of Clairvaux

*Cistercian Monk, called "Last of the Fathers," titled "Doctor Mellifluous" (France: 1090-1153)*

Jesus! How sweet is the very thought of You, giving true joy to the heart; but surpassing honey and all sweetness in His own presence.

Nothing more sweet can be proclaimed, nothing more pleasant can be heard, nothing more loving can be thought of than Jesus, the Son of God.

O Jesus, the hope of penitents, how kind You are to those who pray. How good to those who seek You — but what to those who find!

No tongue can tell, nor can the written word express it: only one who knows from experience can say what it means to love Jesus.

May You, O Jesus, be our joy as You will be our reward. In You be our glory forever.

☩

## St. Albert the Great
*Bishop, Dominican Scholar, Doctor of the Church, Patron of Scientists (Germany: c. 1200-1280)*

*Prayer to Christ in the Blessed Sacrament:*

Hail, thou Saviour of the world, the Father's Word — true victim, living flesh, wholly God, truly man. Ingrafted in thee, may we be worthily offered in thy Majesty's divine temple. Brought nigh to thy Body at thy Father's right hand, may we one day share thine eternity, have fellowship in thy bliss, be incarnate in thine Incarnation, for thine is honour and glory for ever and ever. Amen![40]

✠

## St. Bonaventure
*Franciscan Cardinal-Bishop, Seraphic Doctor
of the Church (Italy: c. 1217-1274)*

Penetrate me, O Lord Jesus, to the bottom of my heart with the sweet and salutary wound of Your love. Fill me with that ardent, sincere, and tranquil love which caused Your apostle St. Paul to desire that he might be separated from his body to be with You.

May my soul languish for You, filled incessantly with the desire for Your eternal dwelling. May I hunger for You, the Bread of Angels, the food of holy souls, the living Bread we should eat every day, the nourishing Bread which sustains the hearts of men and women and contains in itself all sweetness.

May my heart always hunger for You, O most desirable Bread, and feed on You without ceasing. May I thirst for You, O fountain of life, living source of wisdom and knowledge, torrent of delight which rejoices and refreshes the house of God. May I never cease to long for You whom the angels desire to see, whom they behold always with fresh ardor.

May my soul desire You, may it seek You, may it find You, may it tend to You, may it reach You. Be the object of my desires, the subject of my meditations and colloquies. May I do all things for Your glory . . . with love and joy and perseverance enduring to the end.

And be, yourself alone, my hope, my trust, my riches, my pleasure, my joy, my rest, my tranquility, the peace of my soul. Draw me to Your sweetness, Your perfume, Your sweet savor; be to me a solid and pleasant nourishment.

May I love You, may I serve You without distaste and without relaxing in fervor. Be my refuge, my consolation, my help, and my strength. And be my wisdom, my portion, my good, my treasure, wherein my heart may always be — and may my soul remain eternally, firmly, and immovably rooted in You alone. Amen.

✠

## St. Thomas Aquinas
*Priest, Dominican Scholar, Doctor of the Church, Patron of Catholic Universities (Italy: 1225-1274)*

Grant, O Lord my God, that I may not fail in prosperity or adversity, avoiding pride in the former and discouragement in the latter. May I rejoice in nothing but what leads to Thee, and grieve for nothing but what turns away from Thee. . . . Grant me, O my God, to direct my heart toward Thee, constantly to grieve for my sins, and to amend my life. Make me, O Lord, my God, obedient without contradiction, poor without depression, chaste without corruption, patient without murmuring, humble without pretence, cheerful without dissipation . . . serious without constraint, prompt without levity, God-fearing without presumption, truthful without ambiguity, eager in good works without arrogance, correcting my neighbor without haughtiness, and edifying him by work and example without hypocrisy. Give me, O Lord God, a watchful heart, which no curious thought will turn away from Thee; a noble heart, which no unworthy affection will drag down; a righteous heart, which no irregular intention will turn aside; a firm heart, which no tribulation will crush; a free heart, which no violent affection will claim for its own.[41]

✠

## Bl. Angela of Foligno
*Third Order Franciscan, Mystic (Italy: c. 1248-1309)*

O Jesus, You instituted this Sacrament, not through any desire to draw some advantage from it for Yourself, but solely moved by a love which has no other measure than to be without measure. You instituted this Sacrament because Your love exceeds all words. Burning with love for us, You desired to give Yourself to us and took up Your dwelling in the consecrated Host, entirely and forever, until the end of time. And You did this, not only to give us a memorial of Your death which is our salvation, but You did it also, to remain with us entirely, and forever.[42]

✛
_____

# Bl. Margaret Ebner
*Virgin, Dominican Mystic (Germany: 1291-1351)*

Lord, in your highest love and your greatest and sweetest mercy, how they have ever flowed from your eternal Godhead, from heaven to earth, I ask you to preserve our souls in uprightness, our hearts in purity, our lives in true innocence, and all our desires and all our thoughts for our whole life in pure truth. May your boundless mercy prepare us and may your perfect love draw us so that we live in the truth according to your dearest will. And I ask you, my Lord, by your holy sufferings that you forgive all the evil we have done in thought, word, and deed and all the carelessness of our lives. And may the power be given to us to overcome all human evil with ever increasing heartfelt love for you. I desire also that we be given the pure truth by the power of your five holy wounds. May Truth be impressed upon us and may we be led by it so that it may live in us and we in it.[43]

*Prayer before the Blessed Sacrament:*

I ask you, my Lord, to feed me with your sweet grace, strengthen me with your pure love, surround me with your boundless mercy, and embrace me with your pure truth, which encompasses for us all your graces so that they may increase in us and never be taken from us until we enter into eternal life.[44]

✠

## St. Catherine of Siena
*Virgin, Third Order Dominican, Mystic,*
*Doctor of the Church (Italy: 1347-1380)*

[To Jesus Christ:] O eternal Truth,
what is your teaching
and what is the way
by which you want us to go to the Father,
the way by which we must go?
I know of no other road
but the one you paved
with the true and solid virtues
of your charity's fire.
You, eternal Word,
cemented it with your blood,
so this must be the road . . .
Set our hearts ablaze
and plunge them into this blood
so that we may more surely conceive a hunger
for your honor
and the salvation of souls.[45]

*Also by St. Catherine of Siena:*

Eternal God, eternal Trinity, You have made the
Blood of Christ so precious through His sharing in
Your divine nature. You are a mystery as deep as the
sea; the more I search, the more I find; and the more
I find, the more I search for You.

I can never be satisfied; what I receive will ever leave me desiring more. When You fill my soul I have an even greater hunger and I grow more famished for Your light. I desire above all else to see You, the true light, as You really are.

You are my Creator, Eternal Trinity, and I am Your creature. You have made me a new creation in the blood of Your Son, and I know that You are moved with love at the beauty of Your creation.

I know that You are beauty and wisdom itself. The food of angels, You gave yourself to us in the fire of Your love, O Triune God!

✠

## St. Nicholas of Flue
*Husband and Father, Hermit (Switzerland: 1417–1487)*

O Lord God, will to give me
All that leads me to you.
O Lord God, take away from me
All that diverts me from you.
O Lord God, take me, also, from myself
And give me completely to yourself.[46]

✠

## St. Ignatius of Loyola
*Priest, Religious, Founder of the Jesuit Order*
*(Spain, Italy: 1491-1556)*

Take, O Lord, and receive all my liberty, my memory, my understanding, and my entire will, all that I have and possess. Thou hast given all to me, to Thee, O Lord, I return it. All is Thine; dispose of it according to Thy will. Give me Thy love and Thy grace, for this is enough for me.[47]

✠

## St. Peter of Alcantara
*Franciscan Priest, Mystic (Spain: 1499-1562)*

Grant me, O Lord, I beseech you, that I may love you with all my heart, with all my soul, with all my strength, and with all my mind, even as you command. O you who are all my hope, all my glory, my sole refuge . . . O Life of my soul, Rest of my spirit and its joy! O fair bright Day of eternity, and evening Light of my inmost being . . . O Lord my God, prepare within me a dwelling for yourself, that according to the promise of your holy word, you may come to me, and abide within me. . . .

. . . And now since the thing which most pleases you, which most touches your Heart, is that we should have eyes to know and see you, give me those eyes with which I may see you; that is, give me the pure eyes of the dove, eyes chaste and modest, eyes full of humility and love . . . eyes attentive and discreet to understand your will and do it, that, seeing you with those eyes of the dove, I may be seen by you with those eyes with which you did look upon Saint Peter when you did make him to deplore his sin; with those eyes with which you did see the prodigal son, when you went forth to receive him, and did bestow upon him the kiss of peace; with those eyes with which you did look upon the publican, when he dared not lift up his eyes to heaven; with those eyes with which you did look upon the Magdalen, when she washed your feet with her tears; with those eyes with which you did behold your Spouse in the Canticle . . . that, pleasing you with the eye and beauty of my soul, you may grant those adornments of virtues and graces with which I may appear fair in your sight for ever.[48]

✝

## St. Francis Solanus
*Franciscan Priest, Missionary (Spain and South America: 1549-1610)*

My good Jesus, my Redeemer and Friend! What have I that You have not given me? What do I know that You have not taught me? What is my value if You are not with me? . . . You made me and without my asking it. You created me. Turn Your eyes upon me, Lord, and have mercy, because I am alone and poor.[49]

✠

# St. John Eudes

*Priest and Founder of the Congregation of Jesus and Mary and the Sisters of Our Lady of Mercy of the Refuge, Preacher, Advocate of the Sacred Heart Devotion (France: 1601-1680)*

O my God, I give myself to you as my origin; possess me wholly. May I ever remain in you; may I avoid all that may not be worthy of my origin. May you be the beginning and the end of all my actions.

O my God, I give myself to you as my end, my center and my supreme good. Draw me to yourself. Grant that I may continually tend towards you. May you alone be my pleasure, my glory, my treasure and my all.

O my God, I give myself to you as my King. "Give me the grace to do what you command and command what you please" (St. Augustine, *Conf.* 10, 29).

O my God, I give myself to you as my prototype. Imprint upon my soul a perfect likeness of yourself.

I give myself to you as my ruler and my protector. Direct me according to your holy will and preserve me from sin.

I give and abandon myself to you as my sovereign. Do with me what you will.

I give myself to you as my judge. Willingly I submit to all the judgments you have exercised and ever will exercise upon me, in time and in eternity, saying with all respect and submission: "Thou art just, O Lord; and thy judgment is right" (Ps 118, 137). "Yea,

O Lord God Almighty, true and just are thy judgments" (Apoc. 16, 7).[50]

✠

## St. Alphonsus Liguori

*Bishop, Founder of the Redemptorist Congregation,*
*Doctor of the Church (Italy 1696-1787)*

My Redeemer, present in this Most Holy Sacrament, behold me near you: the only favor which I ask of you is fervor and perseverance in your love. I thank you, O holy faith; for you teach and assure me that in the divine Sacrament of the Altar, in that heavenly Bread, bread does not exist; but that my Lord Jesus Christ is all there, and that He is there for love of me. My Lord and my all, I believe that you are present in the Most Holy Sacrament; and though unknown to eyes of flesh, by the light of holy faith I discern you in the consecrated Host, as the Monarch of heaven and earth, and as the Savior of the world. Ah, my most sweet Jesus, as you are my hope, my salvation, my strength, my consolation, so also I will that you should be all my love, and the only subject of all my thoughts, of my desires, and of my affections. . . . Reign, reign, my Lord, over my whole soul; I give it all to you; may you ever possess it. May my will, my senses, and my faculties be all servants of your love, and may they never in this world serve for anything else than to give you satisfaction and glory.[51]

*Also by St. Alphonsus Liguori:*

My Jesus, I believe that you are present in the Blessed Sacrament. I love you above all things and I desire you in my soul. Since I cannot now receive you sacramentally, come at least spiritually into my heart. As though you were already there, I embrace you, and unite myself wholly to you. Do not permit that I should ever be separated from you.

⟊

## Ven. Catherine McAuley
*Virgin, Religious, Foundress of the Sisters of Mercy (Ireland: 1778-1841)*

My God, I am Yours for time and eternity. Teach me to cast myself entirely into the arms of Your loving Providence with the most lively, unlimited confidence in Your compassionate, tender pity. Grant me, O most merciful Redeemer, that whatever You ordain or permit may be acceptable to me. Take from my heart all painful anxiety; suffer nothing to sadden me but sin, nothing to delight me but the hope of coming to the possession of You, my God and my all, in Your everlasting Kingdom. Amen.[52]

## St. Madeleine Sophie Barat
*Virgin, Religious, Foundress of the Society of the Sacred Heart (France: 1779-1865)*

When the love of Jesus is in question, let our generosity know no bounds; we can never bear enough for the God Who suffered so much for us.

Let us love the Heart of Jesus the more, since it is wonderful and forgotten by so many. And if we, favored as we are, give Him but half a heart, what do we deserve?

Love God, and if you cannot meditate, always say, "My God, I love You."

How blind we are! When all earthly love passes away, we entrust ourselves to the loyal love of You, Lord Jesus, our Friend. Amen.

✝

## St. John Vianney
*Diocesan Priest, known as the "Curé of Ars" (France: 1786-1859)*

My Jesus, from all eternity you planned to give yourself to us in this sacrament of your love. Therefore, you planted within us such a longing that it may only be satisfied by yourself.

I may go from here to the other end of the world, from one country to another, from riches to greater riches, from pleasure to pleasure, and still I shall not be content. All the world cannot satisfy the immortal soul. It would be like trying to satisfy a starving person with a grain of corn.

It is good when we set our hearts, our imperfect hearts, on loving you, my God. We were made for charity: that is why we are so prone to love. But we are such that nothing in this world can satisfy us. Only when we turn to God can we be contented.

It happens sometimes that the more we know our neighbor, the less we love him, but with you, O God, it is never so. The more we know you, the more we love you. Knowledge of you kindles such a fire of love in our souls that no room is left for other love and longing.

My Jesus, how good it is to love you! Let me be like your disciples on Mt. Tabor, seeing nothing else but you, my Savior. Let us be as two friends, neither of whom can ever bear to offend the other. Amen.

✠

## Ven. Pauline Jaricot
*Virgin, Laywoman, Foundress of the Society for the Propagation of the Faith (France: 1799-1862)*

It is before your holy tabernacles that my heart dried up by cruel trials has constantly found the necessary strength to bear them; there my struggles have become victories, my weakness courage, my lukewarmness fervour, my perplexities have been changed into light, my sadness into joy, obstacles into success, my desires into the will to accomplish them, my antipathies, jealousies, resentments into burning charity. All I know I have learned at your feet, O Lord; receive therefore the homage of all I am and all that I have, of all I can ever think, say or do that is good.[53]

✠

## Bl. Mariam of Jesus Crucified
*Virgin, Carmelite Mystic (Palestine: 1846-1878)*

I invited the whole earth, to bless Thee,
    to serve Thee.
Forever and always, never to end! With Thy love
    my heart made one.
I invited the entire sea, to bless Thee,
    to serve Thee.
Forever and always, never to end!
I called them, invited them, little birds of the
    air, to bless Thee, to serve Thee.
Forever and always, never to end!
I called, I invited, the star of the morn. Forever
    and always, never to end!
My Beloved, yes I hear Him, He is very near,
    Go forward! Forever and always, never to end!
Open, O curtain that hides Him, I want to see
    Him, my Beloved, to adore and to love.
Forever and always, never to end! With His love
    my heart made one.

I called him, invited ungrateful man, to bless
Thee, to serve Thee, to praise and to love Thee.
Forever and always, never to end.[54]

✠

## St. Katharine Drexel
*Virgin, Religious, Educator, Foundress of the Sisters of the
Blessed Sacrament (United States: 1858-1955)*

*Prayer of Adoration during Exposition of the Blessed Sacrament:*

I adore You, my Eucharistic God. You are there exposed in the ostensorium [monstrance]. The rays are the rays of Your love for me, for each individual soul. If it wasn't for Your love, I would be in hell. I return You thanksgiving through Mary, through St. Joseph, through all the Apostles, Martyrs, Virgins and Sisters of the Blessed Sacrament in heaven. And lastly, I thank You through the sacred host on all the altars throughout the world.

I adore the host which Jesus instituted to be forever the memorial of His death. I adore my Savior who was crucified, dying and entombed on Calvary. . . . I want now to be present in spirit at the bloody death and suffering endured over 1900 years ago. . . .

O Jesus, I adore You in the host of exposition. This act of adoration by union with it is no trivial act, but will with certitude sanctify and transform my soul. I adore Your Heart which desires me to unite myself to Your sufferings.

I thank You in union with the angels and with Mary Immaculate for I am a sinner and not worthy to thank You but I know Your Heart will make thanksgiving for me and will make Your Passion bear infinite fruit both in heaven and on earth, so that the citizens of heaven will receive from them an increase of grace, sinners pardon, and the souls in purgatory alleviation of their sufferings.

The sacred host exposed on the altar gives my soul food for "admiration." I admire my Divine Spouse in His humility but above all His love which has placed Him to be there at the words of the priest at consecration. I admire the love which puts Him at the word of every priest in every century. . . . I know that I am a sinner and a big sinner. I have crucified You many times. I praise You for a love beyond my comprehension and yet You have given me the gift of Infinite love. I glorify You in union with Mary and beg You to make me imitate this love of Yours. . . . Give me the grace to follow Your will in every detail. . . . I must be all His as He is mine.[55]

*Reflection upon the conclusion of Eucharistic Exposition:*

My sweetest joy [is] to be in the presence of Jesus in the holy sacrament. I beg that when obliged to withdraw in body, I may leave my heart before the holy sacrament. When after benediction the priest locks the sacred host in the tabernacle, I beg Jesus to lock me in the tabernacle until morning.[56]

✠

---

## Ven. Charles de Foucauld
*Priest, Hermit (France, North Africa: 1858-1916)*

*From two retreat meditations:*

You dwell, my Lord Jesus, in the Holy Eucharist. You are here, within a few feet of me, in the Tabernacle. Your body, your soul, your humanity, your divinity, your whole being is here in its twofold nature. How close you are, my God, my Saviour, my Jesus, my Brother, my Spouse, my Beloved. You were no nearer to the Blessed Virgin and St. Joseph in the cave at Bethlehem, in the house at Nazareth, than you are to me here now, so often, in the Tabernacle. St. Mary Magdalen was no nearer to you when she sat at your feet at Bethany than I am at the foot of the altar. You were no nearer your apostles when you were seated in their midst than you are to me now, my God.

I am so near to you, so close to you, O my God. Let me serve you here in your presence as I ought, give me such thoughts and words as I should have in you, by you and for you.[57]

✠

## St. Therese of Lisieux
*Virgin, Carmelite, Doctor of the Church
(France: 1873-1897)*

*Prayer to Jesus in the tabernacle, July 16, 1895:*

O God hidden in the prison of the tabernacle! I come with joy to you each evening to thank you for the graces you have given me. I ask pardon for the faults I committed today, which has just slipped away like a dream. . . .

O Jesus! how happy I would be if I had been faithful, but alas! often in the evening I am sad because I feel I could have corresponded better with your graces. . . . If I were more united to you, more charitable . . . more humble and more mortified, I would feel less sorrow when I talk with you in prayer. And yet, O my God, very far from becoming discouraged at the sight of my miseries, I come to you with confidence, recalling that "those who are well do not need a doctor but the sick do." I beg you, then, to cure me and to pardon me. I will keep in mind, Lord, "that the soul to whom you have forgiven more should also love you more than the others"! . . . I offer you every beat of my heart as so many acts of love and reparation and I unite them to your infinite merits. I beg you, O my Divine Bridegroom, to be the Restorer of my soul, to act in me despite my resistance; and lastly, I wish to have no other will but yours. Tomorrow, with the help of your grace, I will begin a new life in which each moment will be an act of love and renunciation.

Thus, after coming each evening to the foot of your Altar, I will finally reach the last evening of my life. Then will begin for me the unending day of eternity when I will place in your Divine Heart the struggles of exile! Amen.[58]

✠

---

## St. Gemma Galgani
*Virgin, Lay Mystic, Patroness of Youth (Italy: 1878-1903)*

Let us join together and go to Jesus in the Tabernacle. Before Him I feel myself as exalting; I am with Jesus, I am before my Love. Thus the Tabernacle opens, the Seraphim bow.[59]

+ + +

Behold me at Your Most Sacred Feet, dear Jesus, to manifest every moment my recognition and my gratitude for the many and continued favors that You have given me, and that You still wish to give me.

However many times I have invoked You, O Jesus, You have always made me happy; I have often had recourse to You, and You have always consoled me. How can I express myself to You, dear Jesus? I thank you. . . .

May your Holy Will be done in all things.[60]

# St. Maximilian Kolbe

*Conventual Franciscan Priest, Founder of the Militia Immaculatae, Martyr in Auschwitz (Poland and Japan: 1894-1941)*

Who would dare to imagine that You, oh infinite, eternal God, have loved me for centuries, or to be more precise, from before the beginning of the centuries?

In fact, You have loved me ever since You have existed as God; thus, You have always loved me and You shall always love me!

. . . Your love for me was already there, even when I had no existence, and precisely because You loved me, oh good God, You called me from nothingness to existence!

. . . For me You have created the skies scattered with stars, for me the earth, the seas, the mountains, the streams, and all the beautiful things on earth. . . .

Still, this did not satisfy You: to show me close up that You loved me so tenderly, You came down from the purest delights of heaven to this tarnished and tear-ridden world, You lived amidst poverty, hard work and suffering; and finally, despised and mocked, You let Yourself be suspended in torment on a vile scaffold between two criminals. . . .

Oh God of love, You have redeemed me in this terrible, though generous, fashion!

. . . Who would venture to imagine it?

Yet, You were not satisfied with this. You knew that no fewer than nineteen centuries would still have to pass from the moment You poured out these demonstrations of Your love to the time I was to be born, so You decided to take care of this too!

Your Heart did not consent to let my only nourishment be the memories of Your boundless love.

You have remained on this forlorn planet in the holiest and most admirable Sacrament of the altar, and now You come to me and You closely unite Yourself to me under the appearance of food. . . .

Now Your Blood flows in my blood; Your Soul, oh God incarnate, permeates my soul, giving it strength and nourishment. . . .

What wonders![61]

✠

## Ven. Maria Teresa Quevedo
*Virgin, Carmelite (Spain: 1930-1950)*

My Jesus, I love you for those who do not love you. . . .[62]

# Meditations

✠

---

## St. Augustine
*Bishop of Hippo, Father of the Church*
*(Africa, Italy: 354-430)*

I will speak, then, to our Lord Jesus Christ; I will speak, and let him hear me. I believe him present; I do not doubt it at all. For he himself has said "I am with you always, even unto the consummation of the world" (Matt. 28:20).[63]

✠

---

## St. John Chrysostom
*Archbishop of Constantinople, Father of the Church (Turkey, Armenia, Cappadocia: c. 347-407)*

*From Homily 24 on the First Epistle to the Corinthians (c. 392):*

When you see [the Body of Christ] lying on the altar, say to yourself, "Because of this Body I am no longer earth and ash, no longer a prisoner, but free. Because of this Body I hope for heaven, and I hope to receive the good things that are in heaven, immortal life, the lot of the angels, familiar conversation with

Christ. This Body, scourged and crucified, has not been fetched by death. . . . This is that Body which was blood-stained, which was pierced by a lance, and from which gushed forth those saving fountains, one of blood and the other of water, for all the world." . . . This is the Body which He gave us, both to hold in reserve and to eat, which was appropriate to intense love.[64]

✝

### St. Francis of Assisi
*Religious, Founder of the Franciscan Order*
*(Italy: 1182-1226)*

I beg you to show the greatest possible reverence and honour for the most holy Body and Blood of our Lord Jesus Christ through whom *all things, whether on the earth or in the heavens*, have been brought to peace and reconciled with Almighty God (cf. Col. 1:20).[65]

+  +  +

I believe that You are present in the Blessed Sacrament, O Jesus. I love You and desire You. Come into my heart.

I embrace You; O never leave me. I beg You, O Lord Jesus, that the burning and most sweet power of Your love absorb my mind, that I may die through love of Your love, since You graciously died for love of my love.

✠

## St. Clare of Assisi
*Virgin, Co-foundress of the Franciscan Order*
*(Italy: 1194-1253)*

. . . Embrace the poor Christ.
Look upon Him who became contemptible for
  you,
and follow Him . . .
. . . gaze upon Him.
consider Him,
contemplate Him,
as you desire to imitate Him.
If you suffer with Him, you will reign with Him.
If you weep with Him, you shall rejoice with Him;
If you die with Him on the cross of tribulation,
you shall possess heavenly mansions in the splendor of the saints
and in the Book of Life your name shall be called
  glorious among men.[66]

✠

## St. Catherine of Genoa
*Widow, Mystic, Hospital Directress, Foundress of the*
*Oratory of Divine Love (Italy: 1447-1510)*

The time I have spent before the tabernacle is
the best spent time of my life.[67]

✠

## St. Angela Merici
*Virgin, Third Order Franciscan, Educator, Religious,*
*Foundress of the Ursuline Order (Italy: 1474-1540)*

*From a biographical study of St. Angela:*

Enlightened by her great faith, St. Angela contemplated her Saviour, hidden under the Eucharistic species, with greater certainty than if she had seen Him with her bodily eyes. She found it difficult to tear herself away from the Tabernacle, where she spent long hours; when the time had come to fulfil her mission, she chose moreover to take up her abode in a small room adjoining the church of St. Afra; after having spent the whole day in prayer and in works of charity, it would be easy for her to go from there to the Blessed Sacrament during the night to pray at length.[68]

✠

## Bl. Peter Favre
*Jesuit Priest, Theologian (France, Italy: 1506-1546)*

On my knees, humbly in the presence of the Blessed Sacrament, I experienced great devotion at the thought that Christ was really present there in body and that, as a consequence, the whole Trinity was present there in a wonderful way that is not found in other things and places. Other things such as images, holy water, and churches bring us in a spiritual manner the presence of Christ, of the saints, and of spiritual powers; but the Blessed Sacrament brings us in a real manner under these appearances the presence of Christ with all the power of God. May his name be blessed![69]

+ + +

O Jesus Christ, may your death be my life; may I learn to find life in your death. May your labors be my rest, your human weakness my strength. May your humiliation be my source of glory, your passion my delight, your sadness my joy. May your abasement be my uplifting — in short, may your sufferings be all I possess. For you, O my Lord, have renewed a life drifting helplessly towards death and you destroyed death.[70]

✠

---

## St. Stanislas Kostka
*Jesuit Novice (Poland, Austria, Italy: 1550-1568)*

*From a biography of St. Stanislas:*

Always previously to entering his class he went to pray before the Blessed Sacrament; and when the lessons were done he might again be seen before the Tabernacle. Willingly, indeed, would he have spent his whole time there.[71]

## St. Lawrence of Brindisi
*Father General of the Capuchins, Doctor of the Church*
*(Italy: 1559-1619)*

The great Prophet of God Moses . . . contemplating the most gracious presence of God in the midst of the Hebrew people in that divine sanctuary of the Holy of Holies . . . had much reason to say: "Neither is there any other nation so great, that hath gods so nigh them, as our God is present to all our petitions" (Deut 4:7). . . .

. . . God has taken our flesh and from that has made Himself a tabernacle far more ample and perfect, not made by the hand of man, but through an act divine: "The Word was made flesh and dwelt among us," whereby is verified most completely that divine oracle: "I will set my tabernacle in the midst of you, and my soul shall not cast you off. I will walk among you, and will be your God, and you shall be my people" (Lev 26:11-12). Not only has this God wished to be with us Himself through the incomprehensible mystery of the Incarnation, God made man in order to make men partakers of the divine nature, but even more incomprehensibly and ineffably through the most divine Sacrament of the altar, in which truly "Our God is present to us" (cf. Deut 4:7). Christ Jesus, Son of God and of the Virgin Mary, true God and perfect man, is contained in this Most Holy Sacrament: "Our God is present to us"; "Behold I am

with you . . . even to the consumation of the world"
(Mt 28:20). . . .

Whoever would wish in full . . . to speak of the
excellence of this Sacrament would need to enter into
that infinite sea of the excellence of God, of Christ. . . .
And all this infinite greatness of God is comprised in
Christ and the whole Christ in this divine
Sacrament. . . ."Our God, our God is present to us."[72]

✠

## St. Mary Magdalen de' Pazzi
*Virgin, Carmelite (Italy: 1566-1607)*

A friend will visit his friend in the morning to
wish him a good day, in the evening, a good night,
taking also an opportunity to converse with him during the day. In like manner make visits to Jesus Christ
in the Blessed Sacrament, if your duties permit it. It is
especially at the foot of the altar that one prays well.
In all your visits to Our Savior, frequently offer His
precious blood to the Eternal Father. You will find
these visits very conducive to increase in you divine
love.[73]

✠

## Bl. Niels Stensen
*Convert from Lutheranism, Bishop, Scientist*
*(Denmark: 1638-1686)*

*From a letter of Bl. Niels written prior to his conversion to Catholicism describing a Corpus Christi procession he witnessed in Leghorn, Italy, on June 24, 1666:*

When I saw the Host carried amid such pomp across the city, the thought came into my mind: either this Host is a simple piece of bread and those who render it such honor are mad, or else It is truly the Body of Christ. In that case, why should I too not honor It? When this idea flashed across my mind . . . I could not persuade myself that so great a part of the Christian world was mad — thinking of the Roman Catholics, among whom there were so many intelligent and learned men. . . .

. . . I spent much time in seeking the truth, trusting to God to open my soul to the knowledge I sought in all sincerity of heart.[74]

✠

# St. Gerard Majella
*Redemptorist Brother (Italy: 1726-1755)*

*From a biography of St. Gerard:*

Gerard's devotion to the Blessed Sacrament was too special, too striking, too beautiful to be dismissed with a word. Literally it can be said that he and his sacramental Lord were lifelong friends. From the moment Gerard heard at [his mother] Benedetta's knee that Jesus was *really* in the church, in the tabernacle, in the ciborium, in the consecrated Host, he drew the logical conclusion with all its practical implications: he should strive to get as near that Presence as possible and remain in It as long as he might. . . .

However, it was when the saint entered religion and became a permanent dweller under the same roof as Jesus that his devotion found its greatest scope and took on its loveliest aspect. . . . Jesus and Gerard were now literally living in the same house: it was a fact as true and plain and simple to him as that Gerard was living in the same house with any one of his own confreres. . . . There was the same instantaneous realization of entering the presence of Jesus when he entered the chapel as there was of entering the presence of his superior when he entered his superior's room. . . .

If Gerard's heart flamed and grew ecstatic before the tabernacle, it suffered and bled at the thought of those who could be there and were not. . . . And so, wherever he went, in town and countryside, he told men of their forgotten Friend. . . . Writing long years after his death, [Gerard's biographer] Tannoia tells us that "it was to him that the populations of many districts are indebted for their assiduity in visiting the Blessed Sacrament."[75]

*"Practice for the Visit to the Most Holy Sacrament" from St. Gerard's "Resolutions":*

My Lord, I believe that you are present in the Most Holy Sacrament. I adore you with all my heart, and by this visit I intend to adore you in all places on earth where you are present in the Sacrament, and I offer you all your Precious Blood for all poor sinners, with the intention also of receiving you spiritually by that act as many times as there are places in which you do dwell.[76]

## St. Benedict Joseph Labre
*Layman, Pilgrim (France, Italy: 1748-1783)*

*From a biography of St. Benedict Joseph Labre:*

Not in Rome alone, but in every city through which he [Benedict] even merely passed, his very ardent love for Jesus in the Blessed Sacrament was well known. He who loves sincerely does not know how to separate from his beloved. Benedict passed the greater part of the day, and sometimes the whole of it, in the churches near his beloved Jesus in His Sacrament, either when exposed for public adoration, especially for the Forty Hours' Prayer, or shut up in the tabernacle; and persons who wished to mention him, and were ignorant of his name, pointed him out as the "Poor Man of the Forty Hours" (*Il povero delle Quarant' Ore*).

. . . In the presence of Jesus the internal fire of his heart shone through his inflamed countenance . . . for his face, when he was not in prayer, being colourless, pale, emaciated, and cadaverous, through his penitential life, it was wonderful to see him before the Blessed Sacrament with a red colour, and often ecstatic and insensible to exterior things. . . .

. . . He prayed in silence, modestly, with his eyes fixed on the Blessed Sacrament, pouring out his affections to that God who does not require us to speak to hear us, but is pleased with the affections of the heart; hence his method of prayer was a good sermon. . . .

. . . From time to time he was afflicted by corporal diseases, particularly in the latter part of his life. . . . So many sufferings did not, however, keep him from visiting the churches, to enjoy the company of his beloved Jesus, to adore Him, and . . . to converse familiarly with Him.[77]

## St. Rose Philippine Duchesne
*Virgin, Religious of the Sacred Heart of Jesus, Missionary
(France, United States: 1769-1852)*

*Testimony of Mother Shannon regarding Mother Duchesne:*

She was gifted with an admirable spirit of prayer and often spent whole nights on her knees before the Blessed Sacrament. . . . One Holy Thursday night she kept me as the companion of her night-long vigil, and she never changed her position, kneeling upright without any support, except to rise to go up to the Repository to trim or replace the lighted candles. At the end of five hours I was overcome by sleep and began to nod. . . . She noticed it and said to me: "Go to bed now. At four o'clock others will come, and I can remain alone until then." She was as alert and wide awake as if it were twelve o'clock in the day.[78]

*April 4, 1806, letter of Mother Duchesne to Mother Barat telling how her aspirations to a missionary apostolate in America were forged during a Holy Thursday night Eucharistic Vigil:*

. . . Your letter came before the night watch of Holy Thursday.

O blessed night! . . . All night long I was in the New World, and I travelled in good company. First of all I reverently gathered up all the Precious Blood from the Garden, the Praetorium, and Calvary. Then

I took possession of our Lord in the Blessed Sacrament. Holding Him close to my heart, I went forth to scatter my treasure everywhere, without fear that it would be exhausted. St. Francis Xavier helped me to make this priceless seed bear fruit, and from his place before the throne of God he prayed that new lands might be opened to the light of truth. St. Francis Regis himself acted as our guide, with many other saints eager for the glory of God. . . .

The twelve hours of the night passed rapidly and without fatigue, though I knelt the whole time. . . . [79]

✠

---

## St. Elizabeth Ann Seton
*Wife and Mother, Widow, Religious, Foundress of the Sisters of Charity (United States: 1774-1821)*

*From a biography of Mother Seton:*

The great central love of Elizabeth's life was ever, of course, the Holy Eucharist. . . .

Elizabeth's room opened off the chapel, and she never ceased to marvel that God allowed her so close to Him: "I sit or stand opposite His tabernacle all day, and keep the heart to it as the [compass] needle to the pole," she confessed in happy wonderment, "and at night still more, even to folly; since I have little right to be *so near* to Him." [80]

## St. John Vianney
*Diocesan Priest, known as the "Curé of Ars"*
*(France: 1786-1859)*

*From the catechetical discourses of the Curé of Ars:*

Our Lord is hidden there, waiting for us to come and visit Him, and make our request to Him. . . . He is there to console us; and therefore we ought often to visit Him. How pleasing to Him is the short quarter of an hour that we steal from our occupations, from something of no use, to come and pray to Him, to visit Him, to console Him for all the outrages He receives! . . . What happiness do we not feel in the presence of God, when we find ourselves alone at His feet before the holy tabernacles!

. . . Ah! if we had the eyes of angels with which to see Our Lord Jesus Christ, who is here present on this altar, and who is looking at us, how we should love Him! We should never more wish to part from Him. We should wish to remain always at His feet; it would be a foretaste of Heaven: all else would become insipid to us. But see, it is faith we want. We are poor blind people; we have a mist before our eyes. Faith alone can dispel this mist. Presently, my children, when I shall hold Our Lord in my hands, when the good God blesses you, ask Him then to open the eyes of your heart; say to Him like the blind man of Jericho, "O Lord, make me to see!" If you say to Him sincerely, "Make me to see!" you will certainly obtain what you desire, because He wishes nothing but your happiness.[81]

✠

## Bl. Pius IX
*Pope (Italy: 1792-1878)*

*From a biography of Pope Pius IX:*

Not content then with visiting frequently the Divine Guest in his private chapel, he always wished, as much while he was Pope as when a bishop, to clean and adorn the altar with his own hand, and this he did with singular taste and sentiments of piety. Once, having admitted into his presence some Religious of the Sacred Heart, giving them salutary teachings and exhorting them to prayer, he invited them to follow him into his private chapel, where the Blessed Sacrament was kept, and said pleasantly: "The poor Pope also has need of remaining a little while alone with Jesus; he has so many things to say to Him, so many lights to ask of Him, so many counsels, so many graces." And having knelt with them, he prayed a little; then having risen he opened the tabernacle, showing them in the interior . . . a monogram of the name of Jesus in diamonds, and said: "Here I place what I have of the most beautiful and precious: all for Him: He is the great Master and Teacher."[82]

✠

## Ven. John Henry Cardinal Newman
*Convert from Anglicanism, Priest, Writer, Apologist*
*(England: 1801-1890)*

The Benediction of the Blessed Sacrament is one of the simplest rites of the Church . . . the Priest twice offers incense to the King of heaven, before whom he is kneeling. Then he takes the Monstrance in his hands, and turning to the people, blesses them with the Most Holy, in the form of a cross, while the bell is sounded by one of the attendants to call attention to the ceremony. It is our Lord's solemn benediction of His people, as when He lifted up His hands over the children, or when He blessed His chosen ones when He ascended up from Mount Olivet. As sons might come before a parent before going to bed at night, so, once or twice a week the great Catholic family comes before the Eternal Father, after the bustle or toil of the day, and He smiles upon them, and sheds upon them the light of His countenance. It is a full accomplishment of what the Priest invoked upon the Israelites, "The Lord bless thee and keep thee; the Lord show His face to thee and have mercy on thee; the Lord turn His countenance to thee and give thee peace."[83]

*From the* Meditations on Christian Doctrine:

God has created me to do Him some definite service; He has committed some work to me which

He has not committed to another. I have my mission — I never may know it in this life, but I shall be told it in the next. . . . I have a part in this great work; I am a link in a chain, a bond of connexion between persons. He has not created me for naught. I shall do good, I shall do His work; I shall be an angel of peace, a preacher of truth in my own place, while not intending it, if I do but keep His commandments and serve Him in my calling.

Therefore I will trust Him. Whatever, wherever I am, I can never be thrown away. If I am in sickness, my sickness may serve Him; in perplexity, my perplexity may serve Him; if I am in sorrow, my sorrow may serve Him. My sickness, or perplexity, or sorrow may be necessary causes of some great end, which is quite beyond us. He does nothing in vain; He may prolong my life, He may shorten it; He knows what He is about. He may take away my friends, He may throw me among strangers, He may make me feel desolate, make my spirits sink, hide the future from me — still He knows what He is about.[84]

✠

## St. Catherine Laboure
*Virgin, Religious of the Daughters of Charity, Visionary of the Miraculous Medal Apparitions of Our Lady (France: 1806-1876)*

When I go to the chapel, I put myself before the good God and say to Him, "Lord, here I am, give me whatYou wish." If He gives me something, I am happy and I thank Him. If He gives me nothing, I thank Him still, because I do not deserve anything more. Then I tell Him all that comes into my mind. I tell Him my sorrows and my joys — and I listen.[85]

✠

## St. Paula Frassinetti
*Virgin, Religious, Educator, Founder of the Dorotheans (Italy: 1809-1882)*

*From a biographical account of St. Paula:*

At St. Onofrio, the Dorothean Motherhouse in Rome, the remains of St. Paula Frassinetti rest in a silver and crystal casket . . . situated beneath the tabernacle of the main altar of that chapel where the Saint had prayed so many hours when her health prevented her from doing more active work. Paula had told her sisters, "I never tire of being near Jesus."[86]

✠

## St. Peter Julian Eymard
*Priest, Religious, Apostle of Eucharistic Devotion,
Founder of the Blessed Sacrament Fathers and Brothers
(France: 1811-1869)*

Before whom am I? You are, Holy Church answers me, in the presence of Jesus Christ, your King, your Savior, and your God.

Adore Him, O my soul, with the faith of the man born blind, when on recognizing his benefactor he prostrated himself before Jesus and adored Him most humbly.

Adore Him with the faith of Saint Thomas and say like him: "My Lord and my God" [Jn 20:28].

But I do not see Jesus like the disciple in the Cenacle; that is true, but our Savior says that they are happier who believe without having seen with their eyes or touched with their hands!

The Church shows me my Savior and my God veiled under the form of a host — as the Precursor showed Him under the form of a simple man, lost in the midst of the crowd, as Mary showed Him to the Magi under the form of a little child.

Adore Him therefore, O my soul, with the faith of the kings of Bethlehem. Offer Him the incense of your adoration, as to your God; the myrrh of your mortification, as to your Savior; the gold of your love and the tribute of dependence, as to your King![87]

✠

## St. John Bosco
*Priest, Educator, Founder of the Salesian Congregations*
*(Italy: 1815-1888)*

Do you want the Lord to give you many graces? Visit Him often. Do you want Him to give you few graces? Visit Him rarely. Do you want the devil to attack you? Visit Jesus rarely in the Blessed Sacrament. Do you want him to flee from you? Visit Jesus often. Do you want to conquer the devil? Take refuge often at the feet of Jesus. Do you want to be conquered by the devil? Forget about visiting Jesus. My dear ones, the Visit to the Blessed Sacrament is an extremely necessary way to conquer the devil. Therefore, go often to visit Jesus and the devil will not come out victorious against you.[88]

✠

## St. Gabriel Possenti (St. Gabriel of Our Lady of Sorrows)
*Passionist Seminarian, Patron of Youth*
*(Italy: 1838-1862)*

*From an account given by one of St. Gabriel's contemporaries in the Passionist Order:*

He was truly enamoured of Christ in the Eucharist. Frequently, he spoke to his companions of his sacramental Lord with an emotion and vivacity so intense that he aroused the enthusiasm of those who listened to him. To Christ in the tabernacle his thoughts instinctively turned, and all the impulses of his heart impelled him to go before the altar to pour out his affections. Many times in the day and night, he would send his angel guardian to visit the Blessed Sacrament when his occupations would not permit him to do so in person. . . .

When out for a walk, if we entered a church, his first thought was to look for the altar of the Blessed Sacrament, and then to kneel before it in silent adoration. . . .

. . . I have often seen him prostrate himself before the tabernacle when he thought no one was near, and pour out all his soul before the Sacramental Christ. At other times, he would become so rapt in adoration during his visits that we had to shake him in order to remind him that it was time to discharge the other duties of our student life.[89]

✠

## Bl. John Baptist Scalabrini
*Bishop, Founder of the Scalabrini Congregation*
*(Italy: 1839-1905)*

Visits to the Blessed Sacrament are a necessity for the heart, which hastens and lingers there where its treasure is. . . .

Pastors must be diligent in cultivating devotion to the Eucharist among their people. Let them go into the streets and bring them into the banquet. Let them invite the rich and the powerful, let them seek out the poor and let them do violence, as it were, to the recalcitrant. They are to prepare their sermons before the Blessed Sacrament, and thus allow Christ to suggest the appropriate words to them. At the tabernacle they must kindle the fire which is to illumine and warm the people. . . .

. . . All should be exhorted to pay a visit to Christ on the evening of Sundays and holy days, and those who live close by should be urged to do so every day. Frequent visits to the Blessed Sacrament make Christ real to us as king and lord, master and friend, brother and spouse. Christ must have first place in the family as in all things.[90]

## Bl. Damien de Veuster

*Priest of the Congregation of the Sacred Hearts of Jesus and Mary, Missionary to the Lepers of Molokai (Belgium, Hawaii: 1840-1889)*

We have established perpetual adoration in the two churches of the leprosarium. It is pretty hard to have regular hours because of the members' sickness. If they cannot come to make their half hour of adoration in the church, I am often edified to see them make their adoration at the appointed time on the bed of pain in their miserable huts. I hope that our brothers and sisters of our beloved Congregation will not mind learning that they have imitators even among the lepers. . . .[91]

---

☩

---

## St. Bernadette Soubirous
*Virgin, Visionary of the Apparitions of the Blessed Virgin Mary at Lourdes, Religious (France: 1844-1879)*

When you pass before a chapel and do not have time to stop for a while, tell your Guardian Angel to carry out your errand to Our Lord in the tabernacle. He will accomplish it and then still have time to catch up with you.[92]

---

☩

---

## Bl. Andre Bessette
*Brother of the Congregation of the Holy Cross, Founder of St. Joseph's Oratory (Canada, United States: 1845-1937)*

*From a biography of Brother Andre:*

All through his life the evening, after his sick calls, was the time he [Brother Andre] devoted to his intercourse with God. When the doors of the church were closed, he went alone or with a few companions into the deserted nave dimly illumined by the flickering flames of the vigil lights. There in the odor of incense and burning wax, he pondered over the woes with which he came in contact. He prayed for all those for whom he had promised to pray: one decade of his rosary for such and such a sinner; one decade for such and such a sick person. Prayer was perceptible on his lips and in the expression of his face. Those who caught a glimpse of him learned what prayer is like when there is something behind the words pronounced. Only when completely tired out did he bring his colloquy with God to a close. . . .

Kneeling on the hard floor, near the Communion rail in front of the high altar, Brother Andre spent an hour, with clasped hands, motionless, plunged in contemplation. Then he made the Way of the Cross. . . .[93]

✠

## St. Frances Xavier Cabrini

*Virgin, Religious, Foundress of the Missionary Sisters of the Sacred Heart (Italy, United States: 1850-1917)*

*A description of Mother Cabrini's Eucharistic devotion:*

In the presence of the Blessed Sacrament, Mother immersed her soul in an ocean of love. She seemed more like a seraphim than like a human being. Indeed, she appeared that way to one of the sisters on a certain feast of the Sacred Heart. After several hours of prayer, Mother had just left the chapel and returned to her room, when a sister spoke to her about something that seemed very important to her. Mother replied, "Let us speak about that some other time. Today, our dear Lord is exposed in the Blessed Sacrament, and I do not want to think of anything else. You, too, stay in the chapel as much as you possibly can. Today is His day. Let us do everything for Him alone."[94]

*Prayer of Mother Cabrini:*

O Lord, Your mercy has urged me to wish to suffer for the love of You, Jesus, and to imitate Your life, which was a continual martyrdom. Give me the desire to humble myself for Your love. Enlighten me how to do so when humiliating occasions present themselves. When I do not feel inclined to follow Your holy inspirations, help me to do so. O Heart of Jesus, by the agonizing abandonment which You experienced in the Garden of Gethsemane, by the horror which You felt when You saw Yourself covered with sins, which made You sweat blood, help me and give me courage to overcome those obstacles which would make less pleasing to You. Yes, yes, O most beloved Jesus, allow me to keep You company in the Garden of Olives. . . . Lord, unite me closely to You; never let me go away from You, my Love; O Heart of my heart, Life of my life! O most comforting sweetness of my soul!

As You have always inspired me, O my God, behold that I offer myself to You today and for all my life as a sacrifice to share Your painful agony in the Garden of Olives; and for the dying, that they may obtain the grace to expire in Your arms, humbly and contritionally for their sins.[95]

✠

---

## Ven. Germano Ruoppolo
## (Ven. Germano of St. Stanislas)

*Passionist Priest, Spiritual Director of St. Gemma Galgani, Scholar of Christian Archeology (Italy: 1850-1909)*

*From a Rule of Life composed by Father Germano for his penitent St. Gemma Galgani:*

Going through the street and passing before any church, I will enter there . . . to make a devout genuflection to the Sacramental Jesus and send Him an affection of the heart.[96]

✠

---

## Ven. Matt Talbot

*Layman, Construction Worker, Third Order Franciscan (Ireland: 1856-1925)*

How can anyone be lonely, with Our Lord in the Blessed Sacrament?[97]

✠

## Bl. Columba Marmion
*Benedictine Abbot, Catholic Writer*
*(Ireland, Belgium: 1858-1923)*

The Church beseeches that we may venerate Christ in the Eucharist. . . .

. . . We show this "veneration" by going to visit Christ in the tabernacle. Would it not indeed be a failing in respect to neglect this Divine Guest Who awaits us? He dwells there, really present, He Who was present in the Crib, at Nazareth, upon the mountains of Judea, in the supper-room, upon the Cross. It is this same Jesus Who said to the Samaritan woman: "If thou didst know the gift of God!"

. . . He is there, really present, He Who said: "I am the Way, the Truth and the Life . . . he that followeth Me, walketh not in darkness. . . . No man cometh to the Father but by Me. . . . I am the Vine, you are the branches; he that abideth in Me, and I in him, the same beareth much fruit: for without Me you can do nothing. . . . He that cometh to Me, I will not cast out. . . . Come to Me all you that labour and are burdened, and I will refresh you . . . and you shall find rest to your souls."

He is there, the same Christ who healed the lepers, stilled the tempest and promised to the good thief a place in His Kingdom. We find there our Saviour, our Friend, our Elder Brother, in the fullness of His almighty power, in the ever fruitful virtue of His mysteries, the infinite superabundance of His merits, and the ineffable mercy of His love.

He awaits us in His tabernacle, not only in order to receive our homage, but to communicate His grace to us. If our faith in His work is not a mere sentiment, we shall go to Him, we shall put our soul in contact, by faith, with His Sacred Humanity. Be assured that "virtue goes out from Him," as of old, to fill us with light, peace and joy.[98]

O Christ Jesus, really present upon the altar, I cast myself down at Your feet; may all adoration be offered to You in the Sacrament which You left to us on the eve of Your Passion, as the testimony of the excess of Your love![99]

Lord Jesus, for love of us, in order to draw us to You, to become our Food, You veil Your majesty. But You will lose nothing of our homage thereby. The more You hide Your Divinity the more we wish to adore You, the more too we wish to cast ourselves at Your feet with profound reverence and ardent love.[100]

+ + +

O Jesus Christ, Incarnate Word, I desire to prepare a dwelling for You within myself, but I am incapable of this work. O Eternal Wisdom! prepare my soul to become Your temple by Your infinite merits. Grant that I may attach myself to You alone! I offer You my actions and the sufferings of this day in order that You may render them pleasing in Your Divine sight, and that tomorrow I may not come before You with empty hands.[101]

✠

---

## St. Leopoldo da Castelnovo
*Capuchin Priest, Confessor (Croatia, Italy: 1866-1942)*

*From the testimonies of several witnesses who knew the saint:*

When he paused in adoration before the tabernacle, he seemed ecstatic. He adored the Most Holy Sacrament even during the night. . . .

Father Leopoldo venerated with particular devotion the Most Holy Sacrament. All the time of which he was able to dispose he spent in adoration before the tabernacle, and always kneeling, notwithstanding his arthritic troubles.[102]

✠

---

## St. Josephine Bakhita
*Virgin, Canossan Sister, a native of southern Sudan freed from slavery and a convert to Catholicism at the age of twenty-one (Sudan: c. 1869-1947)*

[Sister Josephine's] favorite resort was the chapel, where she spent hours in contemplative adoration. . . .

On one occasion, she was left alone, in the chapel, for several hours. A Sister happened to notice it. She approached her and said: "Sister Josephine, how is it? You must have been here for so long. You must be very tired!"

"Not at all!" came the reply. "I have been having a wonderful time with Him. He has waited so long for me."[103]

✠

## Ven. Emmanuel Gonzalez Garcia
*Bishop of Palencia (Spain: 1877-1940)*

*From two meditations:*

The two principal offices of Jesus in His mortal life were those of Saviour and Teacher.

Now, He goes on in the Eucharist exercising the same offices, though in a different way. During His mortal life He saved by pouring out His Blood, and dying, in order to give glory to His Father and life to men — the life of grace here on earth, and of glory hereafter in Heaven. Today in the Eucharist, He continues to save, applying and distributing in silence and invisibly, through Mass and Communion, what He then gained.

At the same time, He is teacher, though with this great difference: that in Palestine He taught by conversation, whereas in the tabernacle He teaches silently. He is silent because many of His teachings, expressed in the words of the Gospel, need, for their thorough rootage in the soul, and their complete growth and fruitfulness, the silence of a tabernacle. Or, more clearly, if Jesus, teaching through the word of the Gospel, awoke a knowledge and a hunger for the great Christian virtues, particularly those unknown to the world, like faith, charity, humility and purity, now, too, by His perpetual silence in the tabernacle, He makes these divine virtues human; by facilitating them; He brings them out clear and fruitful in the life of church and society.

✠  ✠  ✠

Ah, Lord, Your silence and hiddenness in the ciborium are far beyond the comprehension of my passions, which understand nothing but what they can see, touch, taste, by the flesh. Here I am, asking you this madness: "Make me content with You! Let me live content in possession of You!"[104]

✠

## Bl. Elizabeth of the Trinity
*Virgin, Carmelite Mystic (France: 1880-1906)*

When the Blessed Sacrament is exposed in the chapel, the large grille is open. . . . When I open the door to go in, it seems to me that it is Heaven I am entering, and it really is just that in reality, since the One I adore in faith is the same One the glorified contemplate face to face![105]

+ + +

When Our Lord was on earth, the Gospel says "a secret power went out from Him," at His touch the sick recovered their health, the dead were restored to life. Well, He is still living! living in the tabernacle in His adorable Sacrament, living in our souls.[106]

+ + +

O my beloved Christ, crucified by love . . . O Eternal Word, Word of my God, I want to spend my life in listening to You, to become wholly teachable that I may learn all from You. Then, through all nights, all voids, all helplessness, I want to gaze on You always and remain in Your great light. O my beloved Star, so fascinate me that I may not withdraw from Your radiance.[107]

✠
_____

## Bl. John XXIII
*Pope (Italy: 1881-1963)*

Jesus is there, the prisoner of love. Whether the tabernacle be poor or precious, Jesus is always there. The good parishioner of Ars who was surprised by his saintly Curé as he stood gazing silently at the dwelling place of Jesus, his lips not even moving in prayer, replied very simply: "I look at him, and I think he looks at me; and this feeds my soul, gives me strength." So there may be prayer, or even contemplation, in the mere gaze of the eyes.

And we must never forget the visits to the Blessed Sacrament. Modern forms of piety, even when most devout, seem to have less time to spare for this act of homage to Jesus, this keeping him company for a while. Even pious souls are sometimes heard to say: "We live so intensely that we have no time to linger talking with the Lord."

How our soul rejoices when we return to the fervent invocations of St. Alphonsus de Liguori, uttered on his visits to the Blessed Sacrament! The horizons seem to lift around us. About these conversations between God and the soul there exists a whole literature, abundant, modern, attractive and enjoyable. Let us turn to it for our consolation, for the hidden delight of days that sometimes seem lukewarm in fervour and full of uncertainties.[108]

✠

---

## St. Edith Stein (Sister Teresa Benedicta of the Cross)

*Virgin, Jewish Convert, Carmelite, Philosophy Scholar, Martyr in Auschwitz (Germany, Poland: 1891-1942)*

*From a letter of St. Edith Stein:*

As I have just come up from the Chapel where the Most Blessed Sacrament is exposed . . . I would like to bring you greetings from our Eucharistic Savior, and at the same time, an affectionate reproach for letting yourself be led astray by a few printed words about something you have experienced before the tabernacle for so many years. Dogmatically, I believe the matter is very clear: the Lord is present in the tabernacle in his divinity and in his humanity. He is not present for his own sake but for ours: it is his delight to be with the "children of men." He knows, too, that, being what we are, we need his personal nearness. In consequence, every thoughtful and sensitive person will feel attracted and will be there as often and as long as possible. And the practice of the Church, which has instituted perpetual adoration, is just as clear.[109]

## Bl. Pier-Giorgio Frassati
*Layman, University Student (Italy: 1901-1925)*

*From a biography of Pier-Giorgio Frassati:*

From the moment in 1919 when Fr. Cesarini [at the Royal Polytechnic of Turin] founded a university group for nocturnal adoration of the Blessed Sacrament, Pier-Giorgio put his name down and became one of the most fervent and assiduous members of the group. . . .

In the course of the nights of adoration he was noted, not so much for his alertness, as for his faith and devotion. Full of life as he was, he would remain motionless upon his knees on the flagstones all during the long hours of the night. When the adoration was at an end he would tell whoever was going back with him of the deep mystical joy which he felt at the thought of the community of students who were thus rendering homage to Christ in the Eucharist. . . .

It was almost midnight one night when Pier-Giorgio rang the bell at the house of the Fathers of the Blessed Sacrament.

"Brother, I have come to make the students' night's adoration."

"You have made a mistake. Tonight the adoration is reserved for the Fathers."

"Well, then, Brother, let me make it on my own account."

"Go home and sleep, my friend! Do you think it is so easy to watch for a whole night in prayer?"

"Maybe you think I'm not trained for such an exercise? Ah, go on, Brother. Let me in. I won't disturb the Fathers. I'm pretty quiet!"

How could the good Brother resist him? Delighted with succeeding in his request, Frassati entered the church and went into the choir. "After a deep genuflection towards the tabernacle," relates the Brother, "he knelt down in one of the stalls and commenced to pray with wonderful devotion. All the time that I was making my own adoration and he was in the choir, I was struck by his extraordinary deportment and I noticed the many little stratagems he employed to keep awake despite attacks of fatigue. Standing or kneeling, reading his prayer-book, saying the Rosary or looking at the Host, he remained in prayer until 4 o'clock in the morning. He received Holy Communion then and gave an hour to his thanksgiving. At 5 o'clock, the hour when we open the church, he left, his face radiant."[110]

## Closing Reflection

*[The Blessed Virgin Mary] thanks [Jesus] for the Eucharist, and the Eternal Father for this gift. How lonely life would be without it!*

*. . . Keep Our Lord company in the Blessed Sacrament. The disciples asked, "Where dwellest Thou?" They abode with Him all day.*

*In dryness, just stay with Him. Mary will love and adore. "It is good for us to be here," even if attention wanders, like a child with its mother.*

*Our very presence tells Jesus we love Him, even if we are too stupid and too earthly-minded to appreciate and behave properly in His presence. . . .*

*We want to be united with Him, to give ourselves to Him utterly. Our faith tells us He is in the Eucharist: let us seek Him there. If we knew we could find Him anywhere on earth, we would try to go there. We have Him, every free moment, on the altar. Be with Him there. . . .*

— THE SERVANT OF GOD EDEL QUINN
Virgin, Laywoman, Legion of Mary Envoy to Africa
(Ireland, Africa: 1907–1944)[111]

# Appendix 1

*Additional Texts for Eucharistic
Adoration and Reflection*

## Bishop Richard Challoner
*Vicar Apostolic of England (1691-1781)*

*On devotion before Communion:*

Consider that as nothing but pure love brings our Lord to us in this divine sacrament, so the devotion He principally expects of us, when we approach Him, is a return of love. Whichever way we consider these sacred mysteries, we shall find that all things call for our love, and indispensably oblige us to consecrate our whole heart with all its affections to this most loving Lord. His death and passion, endured for the love of us, which we here commemorate; an incomprehensible mystery of love, which will astonish men and angels to all eternity; the wonders He has wrought in this heavenly sacrament, that He might make Himself our food and unite us to Himself; the inestimable treasure He imparts to us; the pledge He gives us of our redemption and of our everlasting salvation — all concur to show forth His love for us, and to claim a return of our whole heart.[112]

# Dietrich von Hildebrand
*Lay Theologian, Spiritual Writer (Europe, United States: 1889-1977)*

From the *Transformation in Christ*:

O Jesus, I know that it is my supreme task to let myself be shaped anew by Thy love; to empty my soul so that Thou shalt rule and unfold therein; and melted by Thy love, to see all things in Thy light, to experience and to do everything in Thy spirit. I know that this reforming of my soul can only come to pass if I lay myself open to Thee, and listen to Thy holy voice. Therefore, at whatever cost, I will be intent above all on providing room in myself for the gentle irradiation of Thy light, and on exposing my heart to the sword of Thy inconceivable love. . . .

Permit not, O Jesus, that my daily obligations make me forget my chief task, that my life be exhausted in the individual works which it is my duty to perform. Thou, Lord, Who hast once said to Martha, "Thou art troubled about many things: but one thing is necessary," grace my soul with holy simplicity, so that it be filled with yearning love of Thee; that I await Thee with burning torches and girt loins; that I stand awake before Thee; and let all else be merely a fruit of this holy life, a superabundance from this inexhaustible source. Set the stamp of greatness and width, of holy freedom and wakefulness, upon my soul. Let my ear never miss Thy voice in the symphony of Thy gifts. Let me never pass over Thy graces with ingratitude, preventing them from bearing ample fruit in my soul. Grant me the fulfillment in my soul of Thy holy word: "Mary hath chosen the best part, which shall not be taken away from her" (Luke 10:42).[113]

✠

---

## The Servant of God
## Rafael Cardinal Merry del Val
*Papal Secretary of State (England, Italy: 1865-1930)*

I salute you, O my Jesus, as my Eternal King and Savior; I therefore enlist myself under your flags, ready to follow you whenever you will call me, and if you are so good to call me to imitate you more strictly and intimately, in poverty, in shame and suffering. . . . I am ready, dear Jesus; speak because your servant is listening, but help me in my weakness.

I desire to live with you spiritually within the Tabernacle, visiting you and adoring you and receiving you spiritually wherever you are present under the Sacramental veil and there at the feet of your Eucharistic Throne to live and die. . . .

O Jesus, I love you, I love you and wish to love you more and more.[114]

+ + +

Make use of devotion to the Blessed Sacrament as a means of persevering in the practice of virtue.

Let us go to Him toward evening and tell Him about our shortcomings, let us ask Him for help and forgiveness. Our Lord loves us, He thinks of us constantly, and His glance follows us every moment of the day.[115]

✠

## The Servant of God Pius XII
*Pope (Italy: 1876-1958)*

*From an allocution of May 31, 1953:*

As the Holy Sacrifice of the Mass religiously offered by the priest with the intimate participation of the faithful, in union with all the Church, is and always remains the great act of Divine worship, so Eucharistic worship is celebrated wherever God-made-man, present in the Blessed Sacrament, is adored even in forms besides that of the Sacrifice. Undoubtedly the Good Shepherd willed to be true bread, as the Angelic Doctor sings in his admirable and profound poems. It is not sufficient for Him that we adore Him: He wills to be our nourishment. . . . But the soul who has understood the love of his Divine Master is not content with a few minutes in which the Bread of Angels rests on his lips; he needs to see again and adore at his ease his Omnipotent Lord, who under the humble appearance of bread puts Himself at his service; he needs to contemplate incessantly that thin veil, which at the same time hides and reveals the love of his Savior; he needs to dwell for a long time before the consecrated Host and take, at sight of God's humility, a position of most humble and profound respect. . . .

Whoever remains often and for a long time prostrate before the Host understands the lesson of the Eucharistic Bread and feels the imperious need of putting that lesson into practice, of completely forgetting himself and of giving himself without reserve to others. By this all men will know that you are Christ's disciples, true adorers in spirit and truth, who glorify the Father by imitating His Son.

. . . The Blessed Eucharist is for Its adorers an inexhaustible source of light and strength. Those who, especially in the silent hours of the night, gather together in adoration with the Angels and render to the Lamb, who was immolated, the thanksgiving due to Him, draw abundantly for themselves and for all the Church waters from the fountains of the Savior.[116]

# Appendix 2

*Scriptural Passages for Eucharistic Adoration*

✠

And he took bread, and when he had given thanks he broke it and gave it to them, saying, "This is my body which is given for you. Do this in remembrance of me." And likewise the cup after supper, saying, "This cup which is poured out for you is the new covenant in my blood." — LUKE 22:19-20

". . . My Father gives you the true bread from heaven. For the bread of God is that which comes down from heaven, and gives life to the world." They said to him, "Lord, give us this bread always."

Jesus said to them, "I am the bread of life; he who comes to me shall not hunger, and he who believes in me shall never thirst. . . .

". . . This is the bread which comes down from heaven, that a man may eat of it and not die. . . . The bread which I shall give for the life of the world is my flesh." — JOHN 6:32-35, 50, 51

I will not leave you desolate; I will come to you. . . . He who has my commandments and keeps them, he it is who loves me; and he who loves me will be loved by my Father, and I will love him and manifest myself to him. — JOHN 14:18, 21

If you abide in me, and my words abide in you, ask whatever you will, and it shall be done for you. — JOHN 15:7

In the world you have tribulation; but be of good cheer, I have overcome the world. — JOHN 16:33

Jesus, Son of David, have mercy on me! — LUKE 18:38

Lord, it is well that we are here. . . . — MATTHEW 17:4

This is my beloved Son, with whom I am well pleased; listen to him. — MATTHEW 17:5

Truly, truly, I say to you, you will weep and lament, but the world will rejoice; you will be sorrowful, but your sorrow will turn into joy. When a woman is in travail she has sorrow, because her hour has come; but when she is delivered of the child, she no longer remembers the anguish, for joy that a child is born into the world. So you have sorrow now, but I will see you again and your hearts will rejoice, and no one will take your joy from you. — JOHN 16:20–22

Come to me, all who labor and are heavy laden, and I will give you rest. Take my yoke upon you, and learn from me; for I am gentle and lowly in heart, and you will find rest for your souls. For my yoke is easy, and my burden is light. — MATTHEW 11:28-30

Behold, the Lamb of God, who takes away the sin of the world! — JOHN 1:29

I am the way, and the truth, and the life. . . . — JOHN 14:6

God has visited his people! — LUKE 7:16

# Appendix 3

*Indulgences for Eucharistic Devotion*

✠

*From the* Enchiridion of Indulgences, *1968, promulgated by Pope Paul VI:*

A *partial indulgence* is granted to the faithful, who visit the Most Blessed Sacrament to adore it; a *plenary indulgence* is granted, if the visit lasts for at least one half an hour [*Enchiridion of Indulgences*, Adoratio Ss.mi Sacramenti].[117]

To be capable of gaining an indulgence for oneself, it is required that one be baptized, not excommunicated, in the state of grace at least at the completion of the prescribed works, and a subject of the one granting the indulgence.

In order that one who is capable may actually gain indulgences, one must have at least a general intention to gain them and must in accordance with the tenor of the grant perform the enjoined works at the time and in the manner prescribed. . . .

To acquire a plenary indulgence it is necessary to perform the work to which the indulgence is attached and to fulfill the following three conditions: sacramental confession, eucharistic Communion, and prayer for the intention of the Sovereign Pontiff. It is further required that all attachment to sin, even venial sin, be absent. . . .

The three conditions may be fulfilled several days before or after the performance of the prescribed work; it is, however, fitting that Communion be received and the prayer for the intention of the Sovereign Pontiff be said on the same day the work is performed. . . .

The condition of praying for the intention of the Sovereign Pontiff is fully satisfied by reciting one *Our Father* and one *Hail Mary*; nevertheless, each one is free to recite any other prayer according to his piety and devotion [*Enchiridion of Indulgences*, "Norms on Indulgences" nos. 22, 26, 27, 29].[118]

# Postscript

✠

## Prayer for the Spread of Perpetual Eucharistic Adoration

Heavenly Father, increase our faith in the Real Presence of Your Son Jesus Christ in the Holy Eucharist. We are obliged to adore Him, to give Him thanks and to make reparation for sins. We need Your peace in our hearts and among nations. We need conversion from our sins and the mercy of Your forgiveness. May we obtain this through prayer and our union with the Eucharistic Lord. Please send down the Holy Spirit upon all peoples to give them the love, courage, strength and willingness to respond to the invitation to Perpetual Adoration.

We beseech You to spread perpetual exposition of the Most Blessed Sacrament in parishes around the world.

We ask this in the name of Jesus the Lord.

Amen.

Our Lady of the Most Blessed Sacrament, help us to spread the glory of Your Son through perpetual exposition of the Holy Eucharist.[119]

✠

## Prayer to Our Lady of the Blessed Sacrament

O Virgin Mary, our Lady of the Blessed Sacrament, glory of the Christian people, joy of the universal Church, salvation of the world; pray for us, and awaken in all the faithful devotion to the Holy Eucharist in order that they render themselves worthy to receive It daily.[120]

# Sources for Texts

✠

1. Terence Cardinal Cooke, *Prayers for Today* (New York: Alba House, 1991), p. 108.

2. Translated from Latin text in Andre Wilmart, *Auteurs Spirituels et Textes Devots du Moyen Age Latin*, Etudes d'Histoire Litteraire (rpt., Paris: Etudes Augustiniennes, 1971), pp. 412-413.

3. From Blessed Margaret's *Pater Noster*, in Leonard P. Hindsley, trans./ed., *Margaret Ebner: Major Works*, The Classics of Western Spirituality (New York: Paulist Press, 1993), pp. 176-177.

4. *Memoriale*, in Edmond Murphy and Martin Palmer, S.J., trans., *The Spiritual Writings of Pierre Favre* (St. Louis: The Institute of Jesuit Sources, 1996), p. 177.

5. Hymn no. 112, "Mille fois mon coeur vous desire," trans. in *God Alone: The Collected Writings of St. Louis Marie de Montfort* (Bay Shore, N.Y.: Montfort Publications, 1987), pp. 539-540.

6. Quoted in *The Life of the Venerable Servant of God, Benedict Joseph Labre*, The Saints and Servants of God [Series] (London: Thomas Richardson and Son, 1850), p. 210.

7. From St. Vincent Pallotti's spiritual notes for a retreat, Nov. 13-19, 1842, in Father Flavian Bonifazi, S.A.C., *Spiritual Thoughts and Aspirations of St. Vincent Pallotti* (Baltimore: Pallottine Fathers Press, 1964), pp. 189-190.

8. *Meditations on Christian Doctrine*, 15, no. 3, in *John Henry Newman: Prayers, Verses and Devotions* (San Francisco: Ignatius Press, 1989), pp. 425-426.

9. *The Book of the Blessed Angela of Foligno*, Part II, Instruction XXXII, in Paul Lachance, O.F.M., trans., *Angela of Foligno: Complete Works*, The Classics of Western Spirituality (New York: Paulist Press, 1993), pp. 298-299.

10. St. Francis de Sales, *Introduction to the Devout Life*, trans. John K. Ryan (Garden City, N.Y.: Image Books, 1966), pp. 118-119.

11. Conference 18, in St. Francis de Sales, *The Spiritual Conferences*, ed. Abbot Gasquet and Canon Mackey, O.S.B., Library of St. Francis de Sales (London: Burns, Oates and Washbourne, Ltd., 1923), p. 353.

12. "Notes from a Ten-Day Retreat," in Sister Irene Mahoney, O.S.U., ed., *Marie of the Incarnation: Selected Writings*, The Classics of Western Spirituality (New York: Paulist Press, 1989), p. 205.

13. Quoted in Sister Margaret Williams, R.S.C.J., *St. Madeleine Sophie: Her Life and Letters* (New York: Herder and Herder, 1965), p. 492.

14. Letter to Francis' niece Marie Libermann, Jan. 27, 1844, in *The Spiritual Letters of the Venerable Francis Libermann: Volume Two: Letters to People in the World*, Duquesne Studies, Spiritan Series 6 (Pittsburgh: Duquesne University Press, 1963), p. 204.

15. Letter of Lent 1853, quoted in Msgr. Baunard, *Ozanam in His Correspondence* (Dublin: Catholic Truth Society of Ireland, 1925), p. 381.

16. Letter of Easter Sunday, 1852, quoted in Msgr. Baunard, *Ozanam in His Correspondence*, p. 358.

17. Quoted in Msgr. Baunard, *Ozanam in His Correspondence*, p. 342.

18. Quoted in Abbé Francis Trochu, *Saint Bernadette Soubirous, 1844-1879* (rpt., Rockford, Ill.: Tan Books and Publishers, Inc., 1985), p. 342.

19. Quoted in Mary Purcell, *Matt Talbot and His Times* (Westminster, Md.: The Newman Press, 1955), p. 151.

20. Archbishop Fulton J. Sheen, *Calvary and the Mass: A Missal Companion* (New York: P.J. Kenedy and Sons, Publishers, 1936), p. 14.

21. Translated from Latin text in *Acta Sanctorum*, July, Tome 3 (rpt., Paris: Victor Palme, 1868), p. 311.

22. From the *Revelations*, in Leonard P. Hindsley, trans./ed., *Margaret Ebner: Major Works*, The Classics of Western Spirituality (New York: Paulist Press, 1993), p. 164.

23. Quoted in Father Gabriel of St. Mary Magdalen, O.C.D., *Divine Intimacy: Meditations on the Interior Life for Every Day of the Year* (New York: Desclee Co., 1964), pp. 612-613.

24. St. Leonard of Port Maurice, *The Hidden Treasure: Holy Mass* (rpt., Rockford, Ill.: Tan Books and Publishers, 1971), pp. 113-114 (with slight modification of the translation — specifically, the replacement of the word "continue" with "remain").

25. Text in *The Life of the Venerable Servant of God, Benedict Joseph Labre*, The Saints and Servants of God [Series] (London: Thomas Richardson and Son, 1850), p. 213.

26. Quoted in Dom Eugene Vandeur, *Adoro Te: Contemplation of the Most Holy Eucharist* (New York: Benziger Brothers, 1939), pp. 155-156.

27. From *A Treatise to Receive the Blessed Body of Our Lord*, in Garry Haupt, ed., *Treatise on the Passion; Treatise on the Blessed Body; Instructions and Prayers*, Complete Works of St. Thomas More, vol. 13 (New Haven: Yale University Press, 1976), pp. 201-202.

28. Maxims, no. 64, in Father Benedict Zimmerman, O.C.D., ed., *Minor Works of St. Teresa: Conceptions of the Love of God, Exclamations, Maxims and Poems of Saint Teresa of Jesus* (London: Thomas Baker, 1913), p. 197.

29. From Anne de Xainctonge's "Directory" for her order, as quoted in Sister Mary Thomas Breslin, U.T.S.V., *Anne de Xainctonge: Her Life and Spirituality* (Kingston, N.Y.: Society of St. Ursula of the Blessed Virgin, 1957), p. 222.

30. Quoted in Breslin, *Anne de Xainctonge*, p. 249.

31. Quoted in Alice Lady Lovat, *Life of the Venerable Louise de Marillac* (New York: Longmans, Green and Co., 1917), p. 143.

32. Quoted in Madame de Barberey, *Elizabeth Seton* (New York: The Macmillan Company, 1927), pp. 142-143.

33. Quoted in ibid., pp. 156-157.

34. From the spiritual notebooks of St. Vincent Pallotti, in Bonifazi, *Spiritual Thoughts and Aspirations of St. Vincent Pallotti*, p. 97.

35. Letter to Madame Catez, Aug. 13-14, 1901, in Conrad de Meester, ed., and Anne Englund Nash, trans., *I Have Found God: Complete Works of Elizabeth of the Trinity: Vol. 2: Letters from Carmel* (Washington, D.C.: ICS Publications, 1995), p. 12.

36. Quoted in Matthew Bunson, Margaret Bunson, and Stephen Bunson, *John Paul II's Book of Saints* (Huntington, Ind.: Our Sunday Visitor, 1999), p. 333.

37. Text in *Hymns to Christ and a Concert of Miniatures* (Middlegreen, Slough, England: St. Paul Publications, 1982), p. 36.

38. Translated from Latin text in *Acta Sanctorum*, July, Tome 3 (rpt., Paris: Victor Palme, 1867), p. 311.

39. Sister Benedicta Ward, S.L.G., trans., *The Prayers and Meditations of St. Anselm* (London: Penguin Books, 1973), p. 237.

40. Text in S. M. Albert, O.P., *Albert the Great* (Oxford: Blackfriars Publications, 1948), p. 129.

41. Quoted in Dr. Martin Grabmann, *The Interior Life of St. Thomas Aquinas* (Milwaukee: Bruce Publishing Co., 1951), p. 64.

42. Quoted in Father Gabriel of St. Mary Magdalen, O.C.D., *Divine Intimacy: Meditations on the Interior Life for Every Day of the Year* (New York: Desclee Co., 1964), pp. 600-601.

43. From the *Revelations*, in Leonard P. Hindsley, trans./ed., *Margaret Ebner: Major Works*, The Classics of Western Spirituality (New York: Paulist Press, 1993), p. 130.

44. Ibid., p. 129.

45. Excerpted from text in Sister Suzanne Noffke, O.P., *The Prayers of Catherine of Siena* (New York: Paulist Press, 1983), Prayer 9, pp. 70-71.

46. Prayer of St. Nicholas of Flue as quoted by Edith Stein in her Nov. 13, 1930, letter to Sister Callista Kopf, O.P., in Josephine Koeppel, trans., *Edith Stein: Self-Portrait in Letters, 1916-1942*, Collected Works of Edith Stein, vol. 5 (Washington, D.C.: ICS Publications, 1993), p. 72.

47. Prayer from *Spiritual Exercises*, Fourth Week, "Contemplation to Obtain Love," in *The Spiritual Exercises of St. Ignatius*, trans. Anthony Mottola (Garden City, N.Y.: Image Books, 1964), p. 104.

48. St. Peter of Alcantara, *A Golden Treatise of Mental Prayer*, ed. G.S. Hollings, S.S.J.E., Tau Series (Chicago: Franciscan Herald Press, 1978), pp. 101, 103-104.

49. Quoted in Fanchon Royer, *St. Francis Solanus, Apostle to America* (Paterson, N.J.: St. Anthony Guild Press, 1955), p. 108.

50. Excerpted from *Interior Colloquies of the Christian Soul with God*, Colloquy 7, in St. John Eudes, *Meditations on Various Subjects*, trans. Father Charles Lebrun, C.J.M. (New York: P.J. Kenedy and Sons, 1947), p. 64.

51. Excerpted from *Visits to the Most Holy Sacrament*, Eleventh Visit, in Father Eugene Grimm, ed., *The Complete Ascetical Works of St. Alphonsus de Liguori: Volume VI: The Holy Eucharist* (Brooklyn, N.Y.: Redemptorist Fathers, 1934), p. 152.

52. Text in Helen Marie Burns and Sheila Carney, *Praying with Catherine McAuley*, Companions for the Journey

[Series] (Winona, Minn.: Saint Mary's Press, Christian Brothers Publications, 1996), p. 39.

53. M. J. Maurin, *Pauline Marie Jaricot: Foundress of the Association for the Propagation of the Faith and of the Living Rosary* (New York: Benziger, 1906), p. 86.

54. Text in Amedee Brunot, *Mariam, the Little Arab: Sister Mary of Jesus Crucified (1846-1878)* (Eugene, Ore.: Carmel of Maria Regina, 1984), p. 46.

55. Text in *Praying with Mother Katharine Drexel — Taken from Her Writings* (Bensalem, Pa.: Mother Katharine Drexel Guild, 1986), pp. 4-5. Text provided courtesy of the Archives of the Sisters of the Blessed Sacrament, Bensalem, Pa.

56. Text in ibid., p. 7.

57. "Retreat at Nazareth," in *Meditations of a Hermit: The Spiritual Writings of Charles de Foucauld* (New York: Benziger Brothers, 1930), pp. 54-55, 38.

58. Text in Sister Aletheia Kane, O.C.D., trans., *The Prayers of Saint Therese of Lisieux* (Washington, D.C.: ICS Publications, 1997), pp. 75-76.

59. Translated from letter of Gemma Galgani to Father Germano of St. Stanislas, C.P., July 27, 1901, in *Lettere di S. Gemma Galgani* (1941: rpt., Rome: Postulazione dei PP. Passionisti, 1979), pp. 193-194.

60. Prayer from letter of Gemma Galgani to Father Germano of St. Stanislas, C.P., Dec. 1, 1900, in Sister Saint Michael, S.S.J., *Portrait of Saint Gemma, A Stigmatic* (New York: P.J. Kenedy and Sons, 1950), pp. 152-153.

61. Text in *Maximilian Kolbe: Stronger than Hatred: A Collection of Spiritual Writings* (New York: New City Press, 1988), pp. 29-30.

62. Quoted in Sister Mary Pierre, R.S.M., *Mary was Her Life: The Story of a Nun, Sister Maria Teresa Quevedo, 1930-1950* (New York: Benziger Brothers, Inc., 1963), p. 187.

63. *On the Gospel of John*, 38, 9, 10, in Barry Ulanov, *The Prayers of St. Augustine* (Minneapolis: Seabury Press, 1983), p. 22.

64. Homily 24 on the First Epistle to the Corinthians, #4, in Father William A. Jurgens, *The Faith of the Early Fathers: A Source-Book of Theological and Historical Passages: Volume 2: Post-Nicene and Constantinopolitan Eras through St. Jerome* (Collegeville, Minn.: Liturgical Press, 1979), pp. 117–118.

65. *Letter to a General Chapter*, in Marion A. Habig, ed., *St. Francis of Assisi: Writings and Early Biographies: English Omnibus of the Sources for the Life of St. Francis* (Chicago: Franciscan Herald Press, 1973), p. 104.

66. Second letter of St. Clare to Agnes of Prague, 1235, in Regis J. Armstrong, O.F.M. Cap., ed./trans., *Clare of Assisi: Early Documents* (New York: Paulist Press, 1988), pp. 41–42.

67. Father Stefano Manelli, F.F.I., *Jesus Our Eucharistic Love: Eucharistic Life Exemplified by the Saints* (New Bedford, N.H.: Franciscan Friars of the Immaculate, 1996), p. 61.

68. Mother Marie de St. Jean Martin, *The Spirit of Saint Angela* (n.p.: n.p., 1950), p. 103.

69. *Memoriale*, in Edmond Murphy and Martin Palmer, S.J., trans., *The Spiritual Writings of Pierre Favre* (St. Louis: The Institute of Jesuit Sources, 1996), pp. 265–266.

70. Ibid., p. 149.

71. Edward Healey Thompson, ed., *The Life of St. Stanislas Kostka of the Company of Jesus* (New York: P.J. Kenedy and Sons, n.d.), p. 63.

72. Translated from "Del SS. Sacramento dell' Altare," in *S. Laurentii A Brundusio: Opera Omnia, Volumen IX, Sanctorale* (Padua, Italy: Offica Typographica Seminarii, 1944), pp. 566–567, 568, 570–571.

73. Quoted in Father Lawrence Lovasik, S.V.D., *The Eucharist in Catholic Life* (New York: The Macmillan Co., 1960), p. 46.

74. From a letter of Niels Stensen to Lavinia Arnolfini, in Raffaello Cioni, *Niels Stensen, Scientist-Bishop* (New York: P.J. Kenedy and Sons, 1962), pp. 70-71.

75. John Carr, C.SS.R., *Saint Gerard Majella* (Dublin: Clonmore and Reynolds, Ltd., 1959), pp. 194, 195, 200.

76. Ibid., p. 101 (English modernized).

77. *The Life of the Venerable Servant of God, Benedict Joseph Labre*, The Saints and Servants of God [Series] (London: Thomas Richardson and Son, 1850), pp. 188-189, 191-192, 193.

78. Quoted in Sister Louise Callan, R.S.C.J., *Philippine Duchesne: Frontier Missionary of the Sacred Heart, 1769-1852* (Westminster, Md.: Newman Press, 1957), pp. 452-453.

79. Quoted in ibid., p. 119.

80. Joseph I. Dirvin, *Mrs. Seton, Foundress of the American Sisters of Charity* (New York: Farrar, Straus, and Giroux, 1962), p. 338.

81. St. John Vianney, Instructions on the Catechism, no. 11, "On the Real Presence," in *The Little Catechism of the Curé of Ars* (rpt., Rockford, Ill.: Tan Books and Publishers, Inc., 1987), pp. 40-41.

82. Translated from Giuseppe Sebastiano Pelczar, *Pio IX e il Suo Pontificato: Volume III* (Turin: Libreria G. B. Berruti, 1911), p. 356.

83. Lecture 6, "Prejudice the Life of the Protestant View," no. 5, in John Henry Cardinal Newman, *Lectures on the Present Position of Catholics in England: Addressed to the Brothers of the Oratory in the Summer of 1851* (London: Longmans, Green, 1899), p. 255.

84. Meditations on Christian Doctrine, 1, no. 2, March 7, 1848, in *John Henry Newman: Prayers, Verses and Devotions* (San Francisco: Ignatius Press, 1989), pp. 338-339.

85. Quoted in Ann Ball, *Modern Saints, Their Lives and Faces: Book Two* (Rockford, Ill.: Tan Books and Publishers, Inc., 1990), p. 138.

86. Ibid., p. 199.

87. *Eucharistic Handbook*, Eymard Library, Vol. 6 (New York: Eymard League, 1948), Part V, pp. 203-204.

88. Father Stefano Manelli, F.F.I., *Jesus Our Eucharistic Love: Eucharistic Life Exemplified by the Saints* (New Bedford, N.H.: Franciscan Friars of the Immaculate, 1996), p. 64.

89. Text in Father Camillus, C.P., *Saint Gabriel, Passionist* (New York: P.J. Kenedy and Sons, 1923), pp. 120-121.

90. Summarized in Marco Caliaro and Mario Francesconi, *John Baptist Scalabrini: Apostle to Emigrants* (New York: Center for Migration Studies, 1977), pp. 257-258.

91. 1879 letter of Father Damien, quoted in Vital Jourdain, SS.CC., *The Heart of Father Damien, 1840-1889* (Milwaukee: Bruce Publishing Co., 1955), p. 203.

92. Father Stefano Manelli, F.F.I., *Jesus Our Eucharistic Love: Eucharistic Life Exemplified by the Saints* (New Bedford, N.H.: Franciscan Friars of the Immaculate, 1996), p. 61.

93. Rev. Henri-Paul Bergeron, C.S.C., *Brother Andre, C.S.C., the Apostle of Saint Joseph* (New York: Benziger Brothers, 1936), pp. 196-197.

94. Quoted in Mother Saverio de Maria, M.S.C., *Mother Frances Xavier Cabrini* (Chicago: Missionary Sisters of the Sacred Heart of Jesus, 1984), p. 293.

95. Text in ibid., p. 45.

96. Translated from "Rules of Life given by Father Germano to St. Gemma," in *Lettere di S. Gemma Galgani* (1941: rpt., Rome: Postulazione dei PP. Passionisti, 1979), p. 462.

97. Quoted in Ann Ball, *Modern Saints: Book Two*, p. 364.

98. Excerpted from Conference 18, "*In Mei Memoriam* (Corpus Christi)," in Dom Columba Marmion, *Christ in His Mysteries* (London: Sands and Co., Ltd., 1939), pp. 356-358.

99. Ibid., p. 357.

100. Ibid., pp. 356–357.

101. Excerpted from Conference 8, "*Panis Vitae*," in Dom Columba Marmion, *Christ, the Life of the Soul* (St. Louis: B. Herder Book Co., 1922), p. 295.

102. Translated from Father Pietro da Valdiporro, O.F.M. Cap., *Il Servo di Dio P. Leopoldo da Castelnovo, Cappuccino* (Padua: Vice-Postulazione di Padre Leopoldo, 1960), p. 82.

103. Maria Luisa Dagnino, *Bakhita Tells Her Story* (Rome: General House, Canossian Daughters of Charity, 1993), p. 103.

104. Bishop Emmanuel Gonzalez Garcia, *Jesus Silent: A Book of Little Meditations*, trans. Sister M. Monica (New York: P.J. Kenedy and Sons, Publishers, 1937), pp. 7–8, 47–48.

105. Letter to Francine Rolland, Sept. 14, 1902, in Conrad de Meester, ed., and Anne Englund Nash, trans., *I Have Found God: Complete Works of Elizabeth of the Trinity: Vol. 2: Letters from Carmel* (Washington, D.C.: ICS Publications, 1995), p. 67.

106. Letter to Madame Angles, Nov. 24, 1903, in de Meester and Nash, *Letters from Carmel*, p. 134.

107. Excerpted from the prayer "O my God, Trinity whom I adore," in Conrad de Meester, ed., and Aletheia Kane, trans., *I Have Found God: Complete Works of Elizabeth of the Trinity: Vol. 1: General Introduction, Major Spiritual Writings* (Washington, D.C.: ICS Publications, 1984), p. 183.

108. Discourse for the Centenary of the Association of the Most Holy Sacrament (the People's Eucharistic League), Feb. 28, 1960, in John Donnelly, ed., *Prayers and Devotions from Pope John XXIII* (New York: Grosset & Dunlap, Inc., 1967), p. 89.

109. Letter to Elly Dursy, May 7, 1933, in Josephine Koeppel, trans., *Edith Stein: Self-Portrait in Letters, 1916-1942*, Collected Works of Edith Stein, vol. 5 (Washington, D.C.: ICS Publications, 1993), pp. 140–141.

110. Robert Claude, S.J., *The Soul of Pier-Giorgio Frassati* (New York: Spiritual Book Association, Inc., 1960), pp. 62-63.

111. Notes of Edel Quinn, quoted in Desmond Forristal, *Edel Quinn: 1907-1944* (Dublin: Dominican Publications, 1994), p. 212.

112. Bishop Richard Challoner, *Considerations upon Christian Truths and Christian Duties digested into Meditations for Every Day in the Year* (London: Burns and Oates, Ltd.; New York: Benziger Bros., 1879), p. 244.

113. *Transformation in Christ: On the Christian Attitude of Mind* (New York: Longmans, Green and Co., 1948), pp. 119-120.

114. Translated from "Morning Offering to God Omnipotent," in Msgr. Pio Cenci, *Il Cardinale Rafaele Merry del Val* (Rome: L.I.C.E.— Roberto Berruti and Co., 1933), pp. 450-451.

115. Text in Father Jerome Dal-Gal, *The Spiritual Life of Cardinal Merry del Val* (New York: Benziger Brothers, Inc., 1959), p. 104.

116. Allocution to the Archconfraternity of Nocturnal Adoration, May 31, 1953, in Benedictine Monks of Solesmes, eds., *Papal Teachings: The Liturgy* (Boston: St. Paul Editions, 1962), pp. 434-436.

117. *Enchiridion of Indulgences: Norms and Grants*, trans. William T. Barry, C.SS.R. (New York: Catholic Book Publishing Co., 1969), "Other Grants of Indulgences," p. 46.

118. Ibid., "Norms on Indulgences," pp. 25-26.

119. From *Eucharistic Holy Hour* (Los Angeles, Perpetual Eucharistic Adoration, 1987), p. 5.

120. Ibid., p. 4.

# Index of Authors Cited

✠

# About the Authors

Internationally known lecturer and retreat master **FATHER BENEDICT J. GROESCHEL, C.F.R.**, is professor of pastoral psychology at St. Joseph's Seminary in New York. The director for the Office of Spiritual Development of the Archdiocese of New York, he is also a founding member of the Franciscan Friars of the Renewal. A prolific author and regular guest on EWTN, he is the founder of Trinity Retreat, a center for prayer and study for the clergy.

**JAMES MONTI** is an experienced researcher and writer on topics of Catholic historical interest. He is the author of Our Sunday Visitor's *The Week of Salvation* (1993) and co-author with Father Groeschel of *In the Presence of Our Lord: The History, Theology, and Psychology of Eucharistic Devotion* (Our Sunday Visitor, 1997). He is also the author of *The King's Good Servant But God's First: The Life and Writings of St. Thomas More* (Ignatius Press, 1997).

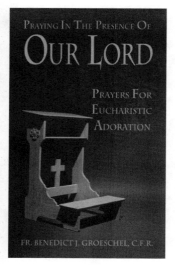